Penguin Elementary Speaking Skills

Teacher's Book

PENGUIN BOOKS

Published by the Penguin Group
27 Wrights Lane, London W8 5TZ, England
Viking Penguin Inc., 40 West 23rd Street, New York, New York 10010, USA
Penguin Books Australia Ltd, Ringwood, Victoria, Australia
Penguin Books Canada Ltd, 2801 John Street, Markham, Ontario, Canada L3R 1B4
Penguin Books (NZ) Ltd, 182–190 Wairau Road, Auckland 10, New Zealand

Penguin Books Ltd, Registered Offices: Harmondsworth, Middlesex, England

First published 1989

1 3 5 7 9 10 8 6 4 2

Edited by Michael Nation
Designed by Mike Brain
Illustrated by Helen Charlton

Set in Linotron 202 10½/12 pt Garamond

Printed in Great Britain by
Hazell Watson & Viney Limited
Member of BPCC Limited
Aylesbury, Bucks, England

Penguin Books

Penguin Elementary Speaking Skills
Teacher's Book

Contents

Introduction

This Teacher's Book gives a key to the exercises as well as the tapescript of the cassette and notes on the presentation and exploitation of each unit. The layout of each unit is identical although there are slight variations in the forms of practice exercises. This uniform pattern is intended to give continuity and a sense of security to the students so they will be familiar with how each unit develops from an early stage. The level of difficulty increases gradually and after every six units a revision unit reinforces what the students have learnt previously.

The units provide a good functional basis for any student who already has some knowledge of English but who wants to improve his/her speaking skills and they practise the skills needed by an elementary learner in his/her contact with English speakers in his/her private and professional life.

The general layout of the book and suggested procedure for the teaching of each unit is as follows:

1 Presentation

    a At the beginning of each unit there is a listening exercise to present the new material to the class. Before playing the cassette elicit from the students any phrases or expressions relevant to the function of the unit that they may already know. In this way the students will draw on their own experience. Write on the board any phrases suggested by the class and briefly discuss their usage and application. This will help to give a general idea of the aim of the unit.

    This exercise always contains a written element where the class have to fill in the missing parts of a dialogue or a table. Each blank space represents a word and there are never more than four blanks in a row. Depending on the level of the class pre-teach any difficult or unfamiliar vocabulary which may cause comprehension or spelling problems.

    Allow time for the students to look at the table/dialogue and then play the tape right through to familiarise the class with the material and tell them not to write anything at this stage. Play the tape for the second time and always ensure that the students have time to fill in the blank spaces which concentrate on the new material and will focus their attention on it. It may be necessary to play the cassette two or three times to give the students time to complete the exercise and when they have finished play the whole tape to let them check what they have written. Go through the exercise very carefully checking what they have done and make sure that all the students end up with the table/dialogue correctly completed.

    b The second part of the Presentation exercise involves using the table/dialogue for controlled oral practice. This is sometimes simply reading through the dialogue in pairs or in other cases using

substitution. It is most important that students have the table/
dialogue correctly filled in (see above) as this provides a pattern and will
start them speaking and using the new material as quickly as possible.
Always make sure that they know how to handle the exercise correctly.

2 Model Phrases

The list of model phrases outlines the new lexis and material for each
unit, most of which will have already been presented in the first exercise.
This list is intended for consolidation and to lay out the new material
clearly for reference. Sometimes the phrases are divided into two specific
functions to avoid confusion (as in Unit 7 Making Offers where they are
divided into 'Offering a thing' and 'Offering to do something').

3 Notes

The notes provide grammatical tips, hints and other supplementary
information on usage which are intended to help the students avoid
common mistakes at this early stage. Before referring to the Notes
discuss points which may have arisen during the Presentation stage and
encourage the class to comment on anything they may have noticed.
Before beginning each unit check the Notes for grammatical points
which may need to be pre-taught in a separate grammar lesson
beforehand. Make all the points quite clear before going on to the other
freer practice exercises where mistakes can occur more readily.

4 Pronunciation

Correct pronunciation not only of individual sounds but also stress is
very important in any language and this exercise is aimed at solving this
problem. It highlights the main structures and involves a simple chaining
technique which can be done by choral repetition and then by small
groups and individuals or, if one is available, it could be done in a
language laboratory. It is not necessary to confuse the students with too
much detail of the intricacies of English pronunciation but more
important to make sure that they say things correctly straight away
before going on to freer practice.

There are lines drawn above some phrases to show:
a a rising intonation:

   Would you like a cup of tea?
b a falling intonation:

   I'm very sorry.

Similarly, where a particular word is stressed in a sentence it is marked
with □:

Oh, how did that happen?

That's really wonderful!

The pronunciation of some words in certain phrases is also given in phonetic script using the IPA.

Can I have a hamburger, please?   [kən]

This is usually used where a word is hard to pronounce or where its pronunciation would vary if it were stressed or not.

5 Fluency Practice Exercises

There are varied fluency practice exercises where students are given a free hand and have to work out correct responses or answers to statements or questions.

a This is generally a table in two columns intended for pair work. One student has to choose a question or statement from the left and the other has to respond choosing a suitable phrase from the right. In most of these exercises there is a variety of possible combinations although not all are suitable and this should be pointed out wherever applicable. Practise one or two examples around the class before starting this sort of pair work exercise to establish the pattern and check that all the students understand what has to be done, and make sure the students take turns at each part. Always go round listening to different pairs and stress the importance of correct pronunciation which has been highlighted in the previous exercise. After the students have done the exercise discuss the possible combinations all together as a class.

b This exercise varies in type but mostly has picture stimuli with pair work practice exercises; any variation is explained in the unit itself. Where a picture is used it is usually in the form of a question or a statement, e.g. A: Would you like a hamburger?, printed over the picture with the response below, e.g. B: Yes, please ... I'd love one.

In these exercises there is always a complete example first and then for subsequent ones part or all of the necessary language is removed. This type of exercise could also be extended by encouraging the students to draw additional illustrations and create exercises of their own.

6 Further Practice

These additional oral practice exercises are not structured and take the form of group/class activities, role plays, discussions, surveys and so on. As well as providing movement and freedom from the constraints of the more structured exercises they use the model phrases in realistic situations which give scope to the students' imaginations. These could be recorded on cassette or video if such facilities are available and then played back to the class to check for any mistakes that may have been made.

7 Situations

At the end of every unit (excluding Unit 10) there is a list of situations where the students have to give the appropriate response. There is a variety of ways in which these can be done. First of all, they could be done in class as a pair work exercise, or they could be done individually round the class where students offer different suggested answers, or as written work at home. The situations could also be used again for revision by referring to them when the students have reached a later stage in the book.

Suggested answers for the situations are included in the notes for each unit.

Unit 1   Meetings and Introductions

The aim of this unit is to give students the necessary phrases and structures they will need when meeting someone for the first time or when introducing themselves to strangers or introducing two or more strangers to each other.

See Introduction for instructions on how to use each exercise.

1 Presentation

Follow the procedure outlined in the Introduction (page 4) about relevant expressions.

There is a series of four short dialogues to present the new material. Check that the students know that they have to fill in the missing spaces and that each dash represents a missing word. If necessary explain the meaning of unfamiliar vocabulary and the phrases mentioned in the tapescript before playing the cassette.

To give variety in the presentation after each short dialogue there is an oral practice exercise. Note that 1a is a pair work exercise; 1b, c, d are to be done in threes.

Where the numbers do not divide in threes either the teacher could take a part or a student could act as a monitor and listen for mistakes made by the others in the group.

After playing through each part of the exercise let the students do the oral exercise while the pattern is still fresh in their minds. If necessary run through the pronunciation of the names with the students and explain the meanings of the jobs (accountant, dentist, etc.).

Unit 1

Meetings and Introductions

1 Presentation

a   Listen to the tape and fill in the spaces:

i

What does Thomas say?	*What does Barbara say?*
Hello, <u>my</u> <u>name's</u> Thomas.	<u>Hello</u>, <u>I'm</u> Barbara.
What does Thomas ask?	*What does Barbara say?*
Where <u>are</u> <u>you</u> from?	<u>I'm</u> from Bristol.
	What does Barbara ask?
	<u>What</u> about <u>you</u>?
	Where <u>do</u> you <u>come</u> from?
What does Thomas say?	
<u>I'm</u> <u>from</u> Edinburgh.	

In pairs make similar dialogues for Chris and Bob, Jane and John.

Name	Town
Chris	Oxford
Bob	Cambridge

Name	Town
Jane	Bath
John	Dover

ii | *What does Jane say?*
This <u>is</u> Maria. <u>She's</u> from Spain. Maria. <u>This</u> <u>is</u> John.

What does John say?
<u>Hello</u> Maria, nice <u>to</u> <u>meet</u> you.
What does Maria say?
<u>Hello</u>, John.

In threes make similar introductions. One person will introduce Evelyn to Henry, another will introduce Stan to Deborah, and another will introduce Trevor to Lorraine.

Name	Country	Introduced to
Evelyn	Switzerland	Henry
Stan	Poland	Deborah
Trevor	Canada	Lorraine

iii | *What does Mary say?*
John, <u>I'd</u> like <u>you</u> <u>to</u> meet Mr Walker.
Mr Walker, <u>this</u> <u>is</u> John Fraser, the <u>office</u> manager.

What does Mr Walker say?
How <u>do</u> <u>you</u> <u>do</u>.

What does John say?
How <u>do</u> <u>you</u> <u>do</u>.

In threes make similar introductions. One person will introduce George to Mr King, another will introduce Sue to Mrs Dunn and another will introduce Fiona to Mr Armstrong.

Name	Job
George Brown Mr King	The new salesman
Sue Mattocks Mrs Dunn	The new designer
Fiona Mr Armstrong	The new engineer

2 Model Phrases

Follow the procedure outlined in the Introduction (page 5) about model phrases.

a Point out the need to use the contracted forms 'I'm', 'What's' in the phrases.

b Discuss briefly the differences between making formal and informal introductions. Point out that to introduce people at a formal professional meeting or when meeting people whose name you would not normally use, it is customary to say 'How do you do'. To friends of your friends, fellow students, etc. the less formal phrases 'This is . . .' and 'Hello, nice to meet you' are more appropriate.

iv | *What does Joan say?*

Mr Snell, I'd like to introduce you to the president,
Mr Rogers ... Mr Rogers, this is Mr Snell.

What does Mr Rogers say?

How do you do, Mr Snell. Nice to meet you. Please call me Roy.

What does Mr Snell say?

How do you do, Mr Rogers. Nice to meet you too.
And please call me Rob.

In threes make similar dialogues. One will introduce Mr Fletcher to Mrs Fraser, another will introduce Mrs Steel to Miss Harris and another will introduce Dr Findlay to Mrs Lawson.

Name	Job
Mr Luke Fletcher Mrs Peggy Fraser	accountant
Mrs Maggie Steel Miss Joy Harris	teacher
Dr Charles Findlay Mrs Heather Lawson	dentist

2 Model Phrases

a Meeting someone new

Hello, I'm Maria.
Hello, my name's John.
What's your name?

Where are you from?
Where do you come from?
I'm from Spain.

b Introductions

Informal:

This is Michael. He's from Germany.

Maria, this is Joseph. Joseph, this is Maria.

Response

Hello, nice to meet you.

Pleased to meet you.

3 Notes

It is a common mistake for students to omit the preposition 'to' after the verb 'introduce' so stress this at an early stage to avoid the problem occurring later, e.g.

'I'd like to introduce you **to** Mr Jones'.

4 Pronunciation

Points to notice are:

a The emphasis should be placed on the name in phrases such as 'My name's Bob', 'My name's Mary', and also the contractions, e.g. 'I'm Fred', 'I'm Jane'.

b The stress on the word 'you' in 'Where are you from?' or 'Where do you come from?' and also that 'from' is not shortened [from] at the end of a question.

c In the phrase 'This is John . . .' all the names are stressed.

d The word 'meet' in 'Nice to meet you' is stressed with a rise in intonation.

e Practise the phrase 'I'd like' very carefully and notice the falling intonation pattern of the name in the phrase 'I'd like you to meet Mr Brown'.

f In the phrase 'How do you do' notice that 'do you' contracts to 'd'you' [dju] when placed in the middle of the phrase.

5 Fluency Practice Exercises

a Divide the class into pairs and explain that each student has to take the part of one of the people in the picture and introduce him/herself accordingly. There is an example given for the first pair of pictures to illustrate the pattern which the students should repeat. Under some pictures a nationality is also given which they should put in their dialogue. Discuss the possible alternatives when the students have done the exercise.

Formal:	**Response**
I'd like you to meet Mr Brown.	How do you do.
Mrs Jones, I'd like to introduce you to Miss Fraser.	How do you do.

3 Notes

a The answer to 'How do you do' is 'How do you do'. It is not a question.

b You introduce someone **to** someone, e.g.:
   I'd like to introduce you **to** Mrs Fletcher.

4 Pronunciation

Now listen carefully and repeat.

5 Fluency Practice Exercises

a Work in pairs for this exercise. Each student take the part of one person in the picture and introduce yourself. We have done the first one for you.

i

ANNA   MANUEL

ii

FRED   CAROLINE

Hello, My name's Anna. What's your name?

Hello, I'm Manuel. I'm from Spain.

iii

HIROSHI   MARIE

iv

TANYA   ALBERTO

/15/

For the second part of the exercise divide the class into threes and tell them that two of the students have to take the parts of the people in the pictures and the third has to introduce them to each other. Some nationalities are given here, too. There is an example given which illustrates the pattern. Tell the students to take turns at introducing and being introduced.

In threes take it in turns to introduce these people to each other. Use this example to help you:

You: Mike, this is Dave.
   Dave, this is Mike.
Mike: Nice to meet you.
Dave: Pleased to meet you.

v

MIKE   DAVE

vi

MRS GRAY   MRS. SMITH

vii

CHRIS   HIROKO

viii

TRACY   DICK

ix

JACK   MARIA

b Divide the class into pairs for this exercise. Point out that the material in each column is not arranged in order and that there may be more than one possible response on the right to a statement from the left-hand column. Monitor the class for accuracy and correct pronunciation while they are doing the exercise. When they have finished discuss the various possibilities they have come up with. Students could repeat the exercise in pairs in front of the class for reinforcement.

6 Further Practice

This group activity is intended to involve all the students and consolidate what they have learnt in the unit. Get the class to stand up and move about the room as if at a formal or informal party and if required give them cards with invented names and information on them. Monitor carefully that correct responses are being given, particularly where formal or informal introductions are necessary. This activity could be recorded on video camera if available or recorded on cassette.

7 Situations

Please refer to the Introduction (page 7).

Suggested Answers

a This is Mike ... he's from London.
b Hello, my name's Joy.
c How do you do ... nice to meet you.
d Hello, my name's Susan and this is my husband, Joe, and our two children, Judith and Annie.
e Hello, my name's Bill. You're new here, aren't you?
f This is Kathy ... I met her on holiday in Spain. These are my parents.
g How do you do.

b With a partner use this table and choose a suitable response. Some sentences may have more than one response.

Hello, I'm Bill. What's your name? I'd like to introduce you to Mrs Peterson. I'm from Madrid ... and you? Hello, Frank, nice to meet you. This is Fiona from Scotland. I'd like you to meet Mr Wickens. This is Tanya from Yugoslavia. I come from Venezuela.	Hello, Tanya. Nice to meet you. I'm from Turkey. I'm Nick. Hello, I'm Judith. How do you do. I'm from Saudi Arabia. Hello, my name's Bob. Nice to meet you.

6 Further Practice

a Introduce yourself to several other students in the group.

b Introduce two other students to each other formally, then introduce them informally.

7 Situations

a Someone new arrives at your school/place of work. Introduce him/her to everyone.

b You are at a party and you see someone you don't know. Introduce yourself.

c You meet an important person for the first time. What do you say?

d A new neighbour has moved into the house next to you. Introduce yourself and your family.

e At school/work you are sitting in the canteen and someone sits at your table. What do you say?

f A friend you met on holiday comes to visit you. Introduce him/her to your family.

g You are introduced to the director of your school/company. What do you say?

Unit 2   Talking about Yourself

The aim of this unit is to give students the essential phrases and lexis they will need in getting to know people in an English-speaking environment. Those studying in Britain or a country where English is spoken will be meeting new people every day and it is essential for them to be able to make new friends at an early stage.

See Introduction for instructions on how to use each exercise.

1 Presentation

a Follow the procedure outlined in the Introduction (page 4) about relevant expressions.

Before playing the cassette explain that two strangers meet in a hotel in Rome. Briefly discuss what sort of things people say about themselves when they first meet and give any unfamiliar vocabulary from the exercise to the class, such as 'accountant', 'engineer', 'hobbies', 'chess', etc. Point out that the names of the speakers are at the top of each column and that the students have to fill in the missing spaces in each column as each person speaks.

b When the listening part is completed divide the class into pairs and explain that they have to use the dialogue as a pattern for the controlled oral practice exercise. Explain that each takes a part and that they must substitute the information given in the columns about the different characters in place of that given in the model dialogue. If necessary explain any unfamiliar vocabulary and do part of the substitution exercise together to make it clear. Carefully monitor the class's performance and where time permits allow one or two pairs to act out the dialogues for the rest of the students. These could be recorded and played back to check for fluency and accuracy in the use of the new expressions.

Unit 2

Talking about Yourself

1 Presentation

a Listen to the tape and fill in the information. Selina and Richard meet in a hotel in Rome.

Selina	Richard
Hello, my name's Selina.	Hello, I'm Richard. Where are you from?
From Canada. What about you?	I'm from England.
Are you here on holiday?	No, on business.
What do you do?	I'm an engineer. What about you?
I'm an accountant. Where do you live in England?	In Oxford. Do you know it?
No, I don't.	It's a lovely town. I live there with my wife and family.
How many children have you got?	Three girls. What about you? Are you married?
No, I'm single.	Oh, I see. Are you here on holiday?
Yes, I am. I'm interested in Italian art.	What about your other hobbies?
Well, I'm very interested in cooking and playing chess.	I see. I like chess, too. Well, excuse me but I must go. I'm going to a tennis match now.
Oh, I'm interested in tennis, too.	

2 Model Phrases

Follow the procedure outlined in the Introduction (page 5) about model phrases.

Discuss briefly with the class their interests, hobbies, jobs, etc., and practise using the phrases, e.g.:

'I'm a banker, I'm interested in travelling and jazz and I like playing tennis and golf.'

or 'I'm a laboratory technician and I like cooking Italian food. I swim in the summer and ski in the winter.'

3 Notes

a Explain that the phrases 'What about you?' or 'And you?' can be used to avoid repeating the same words in a question. This phrase is used a great deal in English for this purpose, not only in these circumstances, so it would be very useful for the students to understand and use it at this stage. When you have been asked a question and have replied and then want to ask the same question back again, 'What about you?' can almost be universally used. Use the short dialogue in the Student's Book as a model for the class to practise substituting a variety of hobbies.

b Emphasise the use of the preposition 'in' after 'interested' and that without it the sentence has no meaning at all. Ask a few questions and get the class to do the same, e.g.:

A: 'What are you interested **in**?'
B: 'I'm interested **in** computer games and collecting stamps.'

b In pairs make similar dialogues for Fred and Pat, Mary and Steve. Use the information to help you.

	Fred	Pat	Mary	Steve
Country	Germany	Switzerland	Brazil	Greece
Job	doctor	chemist	secretary	importer
Married	single	divorced	married	married
Family	three dogs	one son	two children	four girls
Hobbies	cooking	reading	knitting	writing
Sports	cycling	skiing	tennis	fishing
	swimming	tennis	yoga	golf

2 Model Phrases

Questions

What's your name?
Where are you from?
What do you do?
Where do you live/work?
Are you married/single?
What are you interested in?
What about your (other) hobbies?

Responses

I come from Japan/Germany.
I'm from Spain/Brazil.
I'm an engineer/teacher/student/banker.
I live in Tokyo/Athens/Riyadh.
I'm married/single/divorced.
I've got three children/two brothers/a sister/four cats/a canary.
I'm interested in fishing/stamps/classical music/modern art.
My hobbies are cooking/do-it-yourself/collecting coins/reading.

3 Notes

a Note the use of 'What about you?' instead of repeating the question:

    A: What are your hobbies?
    B: I like jazz and swimming ... what about you?
       (Not what are your hobbies?)
    A: My hobby is collecting stamps.

b We always say 'interested in'.
    She's interested **in** astrology.
    Are you interested **in** poetry?
    They are very interested **in** travelling and camping.

4 Pronunciation

Points to notice in this exercise are:

a The country is stressed in the sentence 'I'm from Spain', 'I come from Turkey', and note the short form of 'from' [frəm].

b The pronunciation of 'interested' as [ɪntrəstɪd] and the stressing of the hobby-word in 'I'm interested in computers'.

c The word 'from' is pronounced [from] when it falls at the end of the phrase, as in 'Where are you from?'.

d The word 'you' is stressed in the phrases 'What do you do?' and 'What about you?'.

5 Fluency Practice Exercises

a Divide the class into pairs and tell them they have to work out the missing parts of the dialogue. Explain to the students that picture prompts are given beside the dialogue to help them with the necessary information and remind them to refer to the model phrases for help if they need it. When they have completed the exercise discuss alternative ways of filling in the spaces and, if time allows, tell the class to practise the dialogue again using details of families, jobs, etc. they have made up themselves. Another possibility would be for each pair to write out/draw details of imaginary families, jobs, interests, etc. and then pass them to another pair to substitute in the dialogue.

b Divide the class into pairs and explain that they have to rearrange the phrases in the two columns to make a complete dialogue. Point out that each person in the dialogue chooses from only one column. When the students have completed the exercise ask several pairs to 'perform' the dialogue for the others to monitor. This could be taped or recorded on video (if camera facilities are available) and then played back for general discussion afterwards. Discuss alternative arrangements of the dialogue with the class.

4 Pronunciation

Now listen carefully and repeat.

5 Fluency Practice Exercises

a Work in pairs and look at the pictures. One will be Chris Bell and the other Terry Fletcher and you must make a dialogue. We have done the first part for you. Take turns at this.

① **Terry:** Hello, my name's Terry Fletcher.
Chris: Hello, I'm Chris Bell.
Terry: Nice to meet you. I'm from England. What about you?
Chris:

② **Terry:** What's your job?
Chris:

③ **Terry:** Oh, that's interesting. Where do you work?
Chris:

④ **Terry:** Are you married?
Chris:
Terry: What about your family?
Chris:

⑤ **Terry:** Do you like sports?
Chris:

6 Further Practice

This exercise will enable the students to move around the classroom. First divide them into small groups and tell them to write a questionnaire using the phrases learnt in the unit as a basis. Point out that three sample questions are given and they need to invent three more. When they have completed the questionnaire check that all the students' questions are written correctly and then tell them to interview members of the other groups and fill in their questionnaires. Students who know each other well could give imaginary answers for variety. When they are completed, have a reporting back stage for reinforcement, e.g.: 'Maria's from Bolivia and she works in a primary school. She's interested in collecting shells and playing tennis.'

7 Situations

Please refer to the Introduction (page 7)

Suggested Answers

a My name's Manuel.
b I'm from Portugal/Spain/Brazil.
c I live in Lisbon/Barcelona/Rio de Janeiro.
d I'm a doctor/dentist/secretary.
e I work in a factory/office/bank.
f Yes, I am./No, I'm single.
g I've got two/three children/a wife/husband.
h I'm interested in fishing/stamp collecting/tropical fish.
i I'm interested in tennis/golf/karate.

b In pairs arrange these phrases in order and make a dialogue using alternate columns. Then read it with your partner. We have marked the first three for you.

1	Hello, I'm Chris.	8	I'm a chemist.
11	Have you got any children?	6	What do you do?
15	I play tennis and chess.	10	Yes, I am.
7	I'm a dentist . . . and you?	12	Yes, I've got two boys.
3	Where are you from?	2	Hello, my name's Pat.
13	What are you interested in?	4	I'm from France . . . and you?
9	Are you married?	14	I like squash and folk music
5	I'm from Ireland.		. . . what about you?

6 Further Practice

Make up a questionnaire to find out about the other students in your group. Using the questions in this unit interview several people and then tell the others about them.

	Questions	Names		
		John	Claude	Pedro
i	Where do you come from?			
ii	What are you interested in?			
iii	What about your hobbies?			

7 Situations

a Somebody asks you your name. What do you say?
b Someone asks you where you are from. What do you say?
c Somebody wants to know where you live. What do you say?
d Someone asks you what you do. What do you say?
e Someone wants to know where you work. What do you say?
f Somebody asks if you are married. What do you say?
g Someone asks about your family. What do you say?
h Somebody wants to know what you are interested in. What do you say?
i Someone asks if you like sports. What do you say?

Unit 3   Giving Yourself Time to Think

The aim of this unit is to equip students with a variety of words and phrases which they can readily use when they need time to think how to answer. In one's native language it is often necessary to 'play for time' while thinking about what to say and in a foreign language this is possibly even more the case. In order to avoid long heavy silences this unit is intended to provide a few necessary words to fill the gaps.

See Introduction for instructions on how to use each exercise.

1 Presentation

a Follow the procedure outlined in the Introduction (page 4) about relevant expressions.

Explain to the students that they will hear a series of short exchanges where questions are asked, and before the reply is made a variety of words and phrases are used by the person answering in order to give him/herself time to think. Explain any unknown lexis such as 'return ticket', 'company party', and so on.

b Divide the class into pairs and explain that they have to take it in turns repeating the model dialogues but substituting the alternatives given in the columns under Question and Answer. Practise one or two all together first as examples and point out that in the centre column they must use the Giving Time phrase before they answer.

Unit 3

Giving Yourself Time to Think

Presentation

a Listen to the dialogue and fill in the table. We have done some of the answers for you.

	Question	Giving Time	Answer
i	What's the date today?	Er ...	it's the 27th.
ii	When are you going to Paris?	Just a moment while I check in my diary ...	it's next Friday.
iii	How many people are coming to the party?	Now ... let me see ...	it'll be twenty-four altogether.
iv	How much is a return ticket to London?	Well, I'm not quite sure ...	£10, I think.
v	What's the name of the shop where you bought that book?	Um ... let me think ...	Smiths ... yes, that's it – Smiths.
vi	What time is the football match on TV?	Just a minute ...	it's at 3.45.
vii	Where is the Chinese restaurant?	Er ... I'm not quite certain ...	I think it's on the third corner.
viii	When is the company party?	Just a moment ...	it's on July 21st.

2 Model Phrases

Follow the procedure outlined in the Introduction (page 5) about model phrases.

Ask a few questions of a general nature and encourage the students to practise using the new words and phrases while they think of an answer.

3 Notes

Please refer to the Introduction (page 5).

b Work in pairs and repeat the dialogues with the following substitutions for the questions and answers. Take turns at this.

	Question	Answer
i	When's John's birthday	15th
ii	Rome?	Thursday
iii	to dinner?	eight
iv	to Brighton?	£13
v	that umbrella?	Brown's
vi	film on TV?	8.15
vii	Indian restaurant?	first corner
viii	Jane's party?	May 20th

2 Model Phrases

Umm ... I'm not really sure.

Er ... I'm not certain.

Well, I really can't tell you.

Just a minute / Just a moment while I look / check in my diary.

Now, let me see ...

Uh, let me think.

I'm not quite sure. / certain.

3 Notes

a 'Umm', 'er', 'uh' and 'well'.

These can be used in any situation to give you time to think.

b Just a moment. / minute.

These are often used when you have to look for the answer in a diary, book, timetable, calendar, etc.

c Let me see. / think.

These are used when you have to work out the answer in your head or think carefully about it.

d I'm not quite sure. / certain.

These are used when you don't exactly know the answer to a question.

4 Pronunciation

Points to notice in the exercises:

a 'Just' is pronounced [dʒəst] and the intonation pattern is a gently falling tone, e.g. 'Just a moment . . .'.

b The stress falls on the words 'see' and 'think' and again there is a gently falling tone, e.g. 'Now let me see . . .'

c For this phrase there is a slight rise on 'quite':
'I'm not quite sure.'

5 Fluency Practice Exercises

a Divide the class into pairs and explain that they should take it in turns to do the exercise. One student should ask a question from the column on the left and the other student should select a suitable answer from the column on the right. Explain that there may be more than one possible answer to the question and so it might be useful to do one or two examples with the class all together. Make sure that the students take turns at asking and answering. Afterwards a few examples could be repeated and different answers discussed by the class.

b Before starting this exercise revise numbers, telephone numbers, figures and times and check that the students know how to read timetables, give distances and so on. Pre-teach any unfamiliar vocabulary such as dialling code, further, currency, population, capital and so on. Give the class time to look at the information in the illustrations and ask one or two comprehension questions such as:

'What time does the 0754 train from Dover arrive in Canterbury?'
'What's the dialling code for Argentina?'

Divide the students into pairs and tell them to do the practice dialogues together. (Some of them have been done as examples in dialogue i.) One student has to take the part of A and ask the questions and the other has to respond correctly with the information provided and use a suitable phrase for Giving Time while looking for the answer. Tell them to take turns at this. When they have completed the exercise discuss alternative answers.

4 Pronunciation

Now listen carefully and repeat.

5 Fluency Practice Exercises

a Working in pairs use this table to make short dialogues. In turns one will ask the questions and the other will give a suitable reply. Some sentences may have more than one response.

When's the next train to Brighton?	Er ... it's the 15th.
Where do they live?	Um ... it's just past the bank.
What's the date today?	Just a moment ... it's 10.25.
How much is it?	Let me see ... about an hour and a half.
What's his flat number?	Er ... it's next Wednesday.
When does it begin?	Well, I'm not quite sure.
How long does it take?	Um ... in front of the cinema.
What's her phone number?	Let me see ... in London, I think.
Where is it?	Let me see ... it's 169.
When's your appointment?	Just a minute ... 77071.
What number is it?	Well ... it's about five pounds.
Where can I meet you?	Er ... at 2 o'clock.

b Look at the information in the three sections and then at the dialogues below. Work in pairs, one asking the question and the other giving the answer. Remember to give yourself time to think while finding the answer and take turns at this. We have answered the first question in part i as an example.

i

Train Timetable			
Saturdays			
Dover	0609	0754	0909
Canterbury	0636	0811	0936
Rochester	0731	--	1031
London Victoria	0826	0932	1126

A: What time does the 0609 train from Dover arrive in London?

B: Er ... just a minute ... um ... it arrives at 0826.

A: Is there a train from Dover to Canterbury at about seven o'clock.

B:

A: I want to go from Canterbury to London around nine thirty in the morning ... is it possible?

B:

A: What time does the 0754 from Dover arrive at London Victoria?

B:

ii International Telephoning

Argentina*	010 54
GMT – 3 hrs	Charge band 5A

Australia*	010 61
GMT + 8 to + 10 hrs	Charge band 5B
Adelaide	
Albury	
Ballarat	010 61 02
Bathurst	010 61 90
Brisbane	010 61 79
Melbourne	010 61 3
Newcastle	010 61 49
Perth (W.A.)	010 61 9
Rockhampton	010 61 79
Sydney	010 61 2

Belgium	010 32
GMT + 1 hr	Charge band 1
Aalst (Alost)	010 32 53
Antwerpen (Anvers)	010 32 15
Blankenberge	010 32 65
Brugge (Bruges)	010 32 81
Brussels	010 32 59
Charleroi	010 32 14
	010 32 87
Waregem	010 32 56
Zeebrugge	010 32 50

Brazil	010 55
GMT – 2–4 hrs	

A: I want to phone Australia ... what's the dialling code for Sydney?

B:

A: Is the dialling code for Brazil 010 55?

B:

A: What about the dialling code for Zeebrugge ... that's in Belgium.

B:

A: Is the dialling code for Argentina 010 50?

B:

iii Distances

A: How far is it to Bath?
B:
A: Is it further to Bath or to Bristol?
B:
A: Do you know how far it is to Exeter?
B:
A: Is Exeter in the same direction as Bristol?
B:

iv National Statistics

	Bahrain	Kuwait	Saudi Arabia
Population	400,000	1.7 million	10.8 million
Capital	Manama	Al Kuwait	Riyadh, Mecca
Currency	Bahrain dinar	Kuwaiti dinar	riyal
Language	Arabic	Arabic	Arabic

A: What's the population of Saudi Arabia?
B:
A: Do you know the currency in Bahrain?
B:
A: What's the capital of Kuwait?
B:
A: Do you know the population of Bahrain?
B:

6 Further Practice

Tell the students to make up a list of five questions similar to those in the examples. Explain that they should make questions which require time to think before an answer is given and point out that some helpful phrases are given, e.g. 'holiday two years ago' could be used to make the question: 'Where did you go on holiday two years ago?' Divide the students into pairs and tell them to ask the questions and answer in turns using the Giving Time phrases while they think of the reply.

7 Situations

Please refer to the Introduction (page 7).
To lend more realism to the situations pairs of students could give genuine answers to these and actually look in their diaries and address books or check the local newspaper or a local restaurant menu according to the question.

Suggested Answers

a Um ... let me see ... I think the Italian restaurant is very good.
b Just a moment ... yes, I'd love to.
c Er ... well ... I'm not quite certain because I haven't finished yet.
d Um ... let me think ... go straight on and turn left at the traffic lights.
e Er ... just a moment ... it's 2.30.
f Just a minute while I look ... it was 5 – 3.
g I'm not quite sure ... wait a minute while I go and look.
h Now let me see ... I think I'll have the soup.
i Er ... just a moment while I look.
j Um ... I'm not quite sure ... let me see ... here it is ...

6 Further Practice

Make up a list of five questions like the examples below. Working in pairs ask each other the questions and remember to give yourself time to think before you answer.

a What did you have for dinner last Sunday?
b Where did you go on your birthday last year?

Now make up your five questions. Use these example phrases to help you:

holiday two years ago, get your watch, have your hair cut.

7 Situations

a Somebody asks you the name of the best restaurant in town. Give yourself time to think and then answer.
b A friend asks if you can come to dinner next Thursday. Look in your diary.
c Your boss asks when some work will be ready but you haven't finished it. Give yourself time to think and then answer.
d In the street someone stops and asks for directions to the bus station. You have to think carefully before you reply.
e A stranger asks you the time and your watch is in your pocket. What do you say?
f You're reading the newspaper and a friend asks about the football scores. What do you say?
g A friend from another class phones to ask about the date of the school party. The information is in a notebook so you must give yourself time to find it.
h You're in a restaurant and the waiter asks what you would like to start with. Give yourself time to think.
i A friend phones to ask for your brother's address which is in your address book. What do you say?
j A classmate asks you how to spell a complicated word and the dictionary is on your desk. Give yourself time to think while you find it.

Unit 4 Not Understanding

Students often have problems understanding, particularly at an early stage, and would like to have what has just been said to them repeated or said more slowly to enable them to give a correct response. This unit aims to equip the students with the necessary phrases to ask for this to be done.

See Introduction for instructions on how to use each exercise.

1 Presentation

a Follow the procedure outlined in the Introduction (page 4) about relevant expressions. Discuss the situations in which not understanding might occur, such as when noises interrupt or a person does not speak clearly. Explain any unfamiliar vocabulary in the exercise, such as 'cough', 'crackle', 'bark', etc. Tell the students that they will hear eight short dialogues on the cassette and they have to fill in the missing spaces in the third and fourth columns. Explain that the dialogues appear in the columns from left to right with the question first, followed by the indistinct reply, then the phrase for not understanding and finally the answer. When the students have completed the exercise go over the correct answers with them.

b Tell the students to practise the dialogues in pairs following the pattern in the table and to take turns at this.

Unit 4

Not Understanding

Presentation

Listen to the dialogues and fill in the table.

	Question	Reply	Not Understanding	Answer
i	Could you tell me the time, please?	It's ... achoo achoo ... three	Pardon, I didn't quite catch that.	I said it's half past three
ii	(fast) There's a good film on TV tonight.		I'm sorry, I can't understand what you're saying.	There's a good film on TV tonight.
iii	How much does it cost to send a letter to Spain?	It's ... cough cough ... pence	Sorry?	It's 24 pence.
iv	What's your phone number?	(quietly) It's 66579.	Could you repeat that, please?	It's 66579.
v	Could I have your address, please?	(noise) Yes, it's 146 Rook Road.	Sorry, I didn't catch that.	It's 146 Rook Road.
vi	(crackle) Could I speak to Ms Harris, please?	(crackle)	Could you speak up, please?	Could I speak to Ms Harris, please?

2 Model Phrases

Follow the procedure outlined in the Introduction (page 5) about model phrases.

For further practice the teacher could try asking the class a few simple questions such as 'What's your name?', 'Where do you live?', etc. but interrupt them with a cough or a sneeze or say them very quickly to encourage the class to start using the phrases.

3 Notes

a Explain that any of these can be used when you don't hear something. Notice in particular the word 'Sorry' which can be used in other situations as well as to apologise (Unit 17).

b Point out the difference between 'Could you speak more slowly, please?' and 'Could you speak up, please?'.

c Point out the word 'catch', which in this context is used to mean 'hear'.

4 Pronunciation

Points to note are:

a A slight emphasis on the word 'beg' and the rise in intonation in 'I beg your pardon'.

b The emphasis is on the word 'up' with a rise in intonation at the end in 'Could you speak up, please?'.

c The contracted forms of 'I'm' and 'I can't' and the emphasis on the words 'understand' and 'saying'.

5 Fluency Practice Exercises

a Divide the class into pairs and explain that one student has to say the statement in the left-hand column and the other has to choose a suitable reply from the right-hand column. Where possible the first

	Question	Reply	Not Understanding	Answer
vii	(dog) Where are you going for your holidays?	I'm going to (bark)….	Sorry I didn't quite catch that.	I'm going to Austria.
viii	(music) What would you like?	I'd like… (music) please.	Pardon … could you speak up, please?	I'll have a lager, please.

b In pairs use the table to practise the short dialogues like this:

A: Could you tell me the time, please?
B: It's … achoo … 30.
A: Pardon … I didn't quite catch that.
B: I said it's 3.30.

2 Model Phrases

Pardon?
I beg your pardon.
Sorry?
Could you speak more slowly, please?
Could you speak up, please?
I'm sorry I can't understand (what you're saying).
Could you repeat that, please?
I didn't quite catch that.

3 Notes

a 'Pardon', 'Sorry', 'I beg your pardon':
 These words can be used alone if you haven't heard another person speaking and want them to repeat.
b If a person speaks too fast you can say, 'Could you speak slowly, please?'; or speaks too quietly you can say, 'Could you speak up, please?'.
c 'I didn't quite catch that' = 'I didn't hear that.'

4 Pronunciation

Now listen carefully and repeat.

5 Fluency Practice Exercises

a With a partner use the table on page 22 to practise not understanding. One person will use the column on the left and speak according to the instructions. The other will use the column on the

student should follow the instructions for sound effects, etc. as indicated in brackets and each student has to use his/her acting skills to do the exercise accordingly. Practise some examples with the class before doing it. This exercise could be recorded by the pairs and then played back to the rest of the class with appropriate background or other noises. Point out that the repetition of a phrase is sometimes prefaced by the phrase 'I said . . .'

b Tell the students to write down a list of five questions following the examples in the book. Divide them into pairs and tell them to ask each other the questions in turn. However, one must interrupt the other with a sneeze/cough/other improvised noises or speak quietly/ quickly. The partner must then ask for the question to be repeated using one of the model phrases. Practise the example all together so that the students understand the pattern.

right to give a suitable reply. Then the first person must repeat the statement clearly. Take turns doing this.

i	Her birthday is in January. (Quickly)	Could you speak up, please?
ii	She works in Portugal. (Quietly)	I beg your pardon?
iii	It's going to rain tomorrow. (Sneeze)	Could you speak more slowly, please?
iv	Could I speak to Mr James, please? (Cough)	I'm sorry, I didn't catch what you said.
v	Take the first left, go straight on and then take the third right. (Quickly)	Sorry but I didn't hear what you said.
vi	It's on at the Classic Cinema for two weeks. (Dog barking)	Sorry, I didn't quite catch that.
vii	She's a very good tennis and baseball player. (Quietly)	Could you repeat that, please?
viii	We're staying at the Royal Park Hotel. (Sneeze)	I'm sorry, I can't understand what you're saying.
ix	He always reads *The Times* in the morning. (Quietly)	Pardon?
x	It begins at 7.30. (Cough)	Could you say that again, please?

b Write down five questions to ask your partner, e.g.:

Would you like to go to the cinema tonight?; When's your birthday?; What's your phone number?; What's the date?

6 Further Practice

First discuss with the class the various things necessary to prepare for a class party. Some suggestions are given in the Student's Book. Then divide the class into small groups and tell them to prepare a list of ten things they would need to do and write them down. When they have finished mix up the groups and tell each student to explain his/her list to another student who must write it down. Tell the groups that they must, however, all speak at the same time thereby making it difficult to hear and understand, and so the students must use the relevant phrases to ask for things to be repeated. When they have finished tell the students to check their lists with their partner to see if they are right.

7 Situations

Please refer to the Introduction (page 7). Where appropriate the students could make the sound of coughs, sneezes and other background noises. The students could also make up situations of their own for other members of the group to perform.

Suggested Answers

a Could you speak up, please?
b I'm sorry I can't understand (what you're saying).
c Could you repeat that, please?
d I didn't quite catch that.
e Could you repeat that, please?
f Pardon.
g I beg your pardon.

Work in pairs and ask each other the questions but say each one very quickly, quietly, or with a cough or sneeze so your partner cannot understand. He/she will ask you to repeat the question clearly the second time. Here is an example:

A: Would you like to ... cough ... tonight?
B: I didn't quite catch that.
A: Would you like to go to the cinema tonight?

6 Further Practice

Work in small groups and make a list of ten things you must do to prepare for a class party at the end of term, e.g. buy the food, collect the money, move the furniture, etc. Then work with another group and explain your list of things with everybody talking at once. If it is difficult to understand or you cannot hear you must ask the others to repeat or to speak up.

7 Situations

a Someone is talking to you on the telephone and you can't hear what he is saying. What do you say?
b Your English friend is speaking to you very quickly and you don't understand. What do you say?
c Somebody has just explained the way to the bank but you didn't understand. You want to hear it again.
d A friend is speaking very quietly and you don't understand. What can you say?
e Someone sneezes during a discussion and you don't hear. You want him/her to repeat.
f At the train station you ask about the time of the next train. There are a lot of background noises and you can't hear. What can you say?
g Someone breaks a glass while you are chatting in a bar and you don't catch all the details of the conversation. What can you say?

Unit 5 Asking for and Giving Information

When students are visiting or studying in Britain one of the first things they will probably want to do is ask for information. Asking the way, finding out train times, dialling codes and so on are the kinds of problems encountered in the early days. This unit aims to equip students with the necessary phrases to perform this linguistic function. The unit also covers giving information, which is a useful skill in itself as well as being necessary to understand the answer to a question such as 'Can you tell me the way to the Post Office?'. By practising both asking for and giving information it is hoped that the students will be able both to understand explanations as well as give information if asked.

See Introduction for instructions on how to use each exercise.

1 Presentation

a Follow the procedure outlined in the Introduction (page 4) about relevant expressions and explain any unfamiliar vocabulary which may occur, such as 'dialling code', 'check-in desk', etc. Briefly discuss the kinds of situations when they might need to ask for information and then tell the students they will hear eight short dialogues with questions and answers and they have to fill in the missing spaces in the table. When they have finished check that the table has been completed correctly.

Unit 5

Asking for and Giving Information

~~re~~sentation

~~L~~isten to the tape and fill in the spaces:

Question	Answer
Excuse me, could you tell me the time, please?	Yes, of course. It's 10.15.
Excuse me, do you know when the bank opens?	Yes, it opens at 9.30.
Excuse me, can you tell me where the cinema is?	Yes, go straight on, it's on your right.
Hello, can you tell me the dialling code for Brighton, please?	Yes, it's 0273.
Do you know where the BA check-in desk is?	No, I'm afraid I don't.
Excuse me, could you tell me where I could buy a postcard near here, please?	Yes, in the little shop there on the corner.
Excuse me, do you know where the bank is?	Sorry, no. I'm a stranger here myself.
Excuse me, can you tell me when the supermarket opens?	Yes, of course. It opens at 8.30 every morning.

b Below the table is a controlled oral practice exercise to be done in pairs in which the students have to use the new material. Tell the class to refer to the table for guidance and if necessary do one or two examples together for practice. Pre-teach such phrases as 'on the right', 'on the left', 'round the corner', etc. The list of situations that was written on the board before playing the tape could be used for sample dialogues. Then practise the nine situations for asking for and giving information. Monitor carefully for correct use of the phrases and answers and discuss the various possibilities afterwards.

2 Model Phrases

Follow the procedure outlined in the Introduction (page 5) about model phrases. Discuss briefly with the class any other situations where asking for and giving information occurs and practise using the phrases, e.g.:

'Excuse me, can you tell me when the lesson ends?'
'Excuse me, could you tell me the way to the bus station?', etc.

using local times and places.

b Work in pairs and ask similar questions. Use the information below
to help you with the questions and answers.

	Questions	Answers
i	Time	2.30
ii	When the supermarket opens.	You don't know.

iii   Where the bus station is
(you are at X).

iv   Dialling code for London.   01

v   Where the TWA check-in desk is
(you are at X).

vi	Where to buy stamps.	At the Post Office.
vii	Where the chemist's is.	Beside the bank on the corner.
viii	When the Post Office opens.	You don't know.

ix   Where a post box is
(you are at X).

2 Model Phrases

a Asking for Information

Excuse me,   can you tell me the time, please?
could you tell me the way to Oxford Street, please?
do you know the time of the next train to London,
please?
do you know where the Post Office is, please?

3 Notes

Use the diagrams to illustrate the various directions and explain the words 'turning', 'crossroads', 'corner' and so on. Emphasise the various prepositions used, e.g. **'on** the right/left', **'at** the crossroads', **'at** the corner'.

b Giving Information

Yes, of course. It's 3 o'clock.
Go straight along until the third corner.

Yes, it leaves at 4.15.
it's just past the bank on the right.

No, I'm afraid I can't.

No, I'm sorry I don't.

Sorry, no.

3 Notes

a 'Excuse me' is used   i to start a conversation;
                       ii to speak to someone you don't know;
                      iii to attract attention before a question.

b On the telephone it is not necessary to say 'Excuse me' first.

c Negative responses:

In negative responses we do not repeat the information, it sounds a little rude. Use the first verb only, e.g.:

Response

i Can you tell me the time of the next bus, please?   No, I'm afraid I can't.

ii Do you know where the bus station is?   No, I'm afraid I don't.

d Directions

i Go straight on.

ii Take the first turning on the right.

iii Take the second turning on the left.

iv Turn left at the crossroads.

4 Pronunciation

Points to note are:

a The syllable stress in 'Excuse me'. The emphasis on the word 'time'.

b The emphasis on the word 'cinema' in the phrase 'Do you know where the cinema is?' This could be practised by substituting other words such as 'hospital', 'school', 'post office', 'bank', etc.

c In the phrase 'Of course' the word 'of' is pronounced [əv].

d In directions note the emphasis on 'straight' and 'left'.

e The contractions 'I'm afraid' and 'I'm sorry' [aɪm].

5 Fluency Practice Exercises

a Divide the class into pairs and explain that they should ask and answer alternately. The questions are in the left-hand column and the answers are on the right, and there may be several possible answers. Tell each student to cover over the column he/she is not using. Discuss the various alternatives when they have finished.

v Turn right at the third corner.

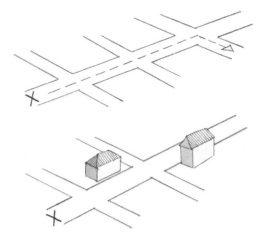

vi It's on the left-hand side.
    right-hand side.

4 Pronunciation

Now listen carefully and repeat.

5 Fluency Practice Exercises

a With a partner use the table to ask for information and either give it or
don't give it. One will use the column on the left to ask for
information and the other will reply from the column on the right.
Some sentences may have more than one response. Take turns at this.

Excuse me, can you tell me where the shoe department is, please?	Go straight on and turn right at the corner.
Could you tell me the way to Waterloo Station, please?	Yes, it's on the second floor.
Do you know the phone number of the Albert Hall?	Yes, it's at 6.35.
Do you know how far it is to the Post Office?	Yes, it's 01–866–4921.
Do you know the time of the next train?	No, I'm afraid I can't.
Can you tell me the time, please?	No, I'm sorry I don't.
Could you tell me where the bank is, please?	I'm sorry but I don't know.
Do you know where I can buy a film?	It's beside the cinema in the town centre.
Could you tell me the exchange rate for dollars, please?	It's on the third corner – you can't miss it.
Do you know if the supermarket is open on Saturday afternoon?	Yes, it's only a few minutes from here.

b Divide the students into pairs and tell them they have to ask for and give directions in turn. Point out that the questions are given and that they are always at the point marked X on the maps. Tell them to read the example together first for practice.

b Work in pairs. One student will ask the way to the place marked and the other will give the directions. Take turns at this. We have done the first one for you. (You are at X.)

    i A: Excuse me, could you tell me where the bank is, please?

       B: Yes, certainly . . . take the first turning on the right and it's on the right.

    ii A: Excuse me, do you know where the Post Office is?

       B: _____

    iii A: Can you tell me the way to the Chinese restaurant?

       B: _____

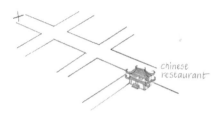

    iv A: Excuse me, do you know if there is a shoe shop near here?

       B: _____

    v A: Could you tell me where I could find a bookshop?

       B: _____

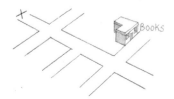

6 Further Practice

a Directions

Divide the class into pairs and allocate one of the maps (Map 1 or Map 2) to each student. Tell them to mark their four places on the relevant map anywhere they like, e.g.:

Student A   Map 1   places A–D
Student B   Map 2   places E–H

Student A must ask the way from point X to the four places Student B has marked on Map 2 and he/she will give the appropriate directions. Student A should then mark the four places on his/her blank map and vice versa. When they have finished the students should compare their respective maps to check that they have given the correct directions.

b Telephoning

Divide the class into pairs and explain that one is the caller and the other is the telephonist. Tell them to cover up the column which does not refer to them and then the caller must ask the questions which the telephonist must answer. Tell the caller to write down the numbers he/she hears from the telephonist as they go along so they can be checked afterwards. To lend greater realism use a telephone book or a set of real numbers and places where possible as supplementary material. So that each student has a chance to practise they could do half each or repeat the exercise with the telephonist giving his/her own invented answers.

6 Further Practice

a Directions

Work in pairs. Student 1 will mark places A – D on Map 1 and student 2 will mark places E – H on Map 2. Do not look at the other student's map. Take turns asking each other the way and giving directions: (you are at X).

e.g. student 1: Excuse me, can you tell me the way to the Post Office?
   student 2: Do you know where the bank is, please?

Map 1

A = cinema
B = bank
C = station
D = Park Hotel

Map 2

E = Post Office
F = bookshop
G = café
H = restaurant

b Telephone

Work in pairs – one as the caller and the other as the telephonist. The caller will ask for the information and the telephonist will give it. Look only at your part and cover up the other one. Take turns at this.

	Caller	Telephonist
i	Dialling code for Paris	010 331
ii	Number of the Speaking Clock	8081
iii	Dialling code for Tokyo	010 813
iv	Number of the Park Hotel	93 87777
v	The weather forecast	93 8092
vi	The sports results	93 8020
vii	British Museum	01 580 1110
viii	Daily horoscope	01 246 8000
ix	Number of the Chinese Restaurant	76601
x	Number of the bus station	911546
xi	Number of the bank	34025

7 Situations

Please refer to the Introduction (page 7).

Suggested Answers

a Could you tell me the time, please?
b Excuse me, could you tell me the way to the supermarket, please?
c I'm sorry but I don't know.
d Could you tell me the dialling code for Venice/Lima/Riyadh/Osaka?
e How much is a letter to Brazil?
f You go straight along until the second corner and turn left; it's on the right opposite the bank.
g Could you tell me what's on at the (Classic/Odeon/Regency) cinema?
h Excuse me, could you tell me about digital watches, please?
i Excuse me, do you know the time of the next train to London, please?
j Could you tell me the exchange rate for yen/marks/lire/francs/pesos?
k Could you tell me about the different starters, please?
l Excuse me, do you know where I can buy a film for my camera?

7 Situations

  a Ask somebody the time.

  b Ask the way to the supermarket.

  c You are a visitor in town and someone asks you the way to the bus station. You don't know.

  d Call Directory Enquiries and ask for the dialling code for your town.

  e At the Post Office you want to send a letter to Brazil. Ask how much it costs.

  f Explain the way from your house to the nearest letter box.

  g Ask someone what's on at the local cinema. He/she doesn't know.

  h You are in a jewellery shop and want to buy a watch. Ask the assistant for help.

  i At the railway station ask the time of the next train to London.

  j At the bank ask about the exchange rate for your currency.

  k In a restaurant ask the waiter to explain the different starters.

  l Explain where to buy a film for a camera.

Unit 6 Asking for Things
Part A Food and Drink

This unit is divided into two parts:
Part A is concerned with Food and Drink in restaurants, cafés, bars, etc.
Part B is concerned with Shops and Services.

The lay-out of each part is the same as for a whole unit, so where lesson time is limited it could be treated as two separate units.

See Introduction for instructions on how to use each exercise.

1 Presentation

a Follow the procedure outlined in the Introduction (page 4) about relevant expressions. Explain that this part is about asking for things to eat and drink and give the students any unfamiliar vocabulary which may occur in the table, e.g. 'crisps', 'salad dressing', etc. Then tell the class they will hear eight short dialogues in which people are asking for things to eat and drink and that they have to fill in the table accordingly. In some cases not all the dialogue, only the key phrases, is reproduced.

b Tell the students to practise the dialogues in pairs. One student has to repeat the completed first two columns and the other has to reply from the third column. Check carefully that the students understand what they have to do and make sure they ask and answer correctly.

Unit 6

Asking for Things

Part A   Food and Drink

Presentation

Listen to the tape and fill in the spaces:

	Asking Phrases	What	Reply
i	I'd like	a cup of coffee, please.	Yes, certainly, sir.
ii	I'll have	chicken and chips, please.	Certainly.
iii	Can I have	two Cokes, please?	Yes, of course. Here you are.
iv	Could I have	a hamburger, please?	Yes, certainly. Anything else?
v	Could you pass me	the butter, please?	Yes, of course. Here you are.
vi	I'd like	a packet of peanuts, please. Umm . . . a packet of crisps, too, please.	Here you are. Anything else? Certainly.
vii	Could I have	chocolate ice cream, please?	Yes, of course.
viii	Could you pass	the salad dressing, please?	Certainly. Here it is.

In pairs repeat these short dialogues. One will ask and the other will reply and then change around.

2 Model Phrases

Follow the procedure outlined in the Introduction (page 5) about model phrases.

Note that 'can' and 'could' are virtually interchangeable.

3 Notes

a Point out that this phrase need not only be used for food but also for other things, e.g. 'a book', 'an ashtray', 'a pen', etc. and that the 'me' is optional.

b Tell the class that this phrase is used to give something to someone and it need not only be food or drink.

4 Pronunciation

Points to note are:

a The contracted forms 'I'd' [aɪd] and 'I'll' [aɪl].
b The pronunciation of 'can' [kən] in 'Can I have ...'
c The emphasis which falls on the thing required (i.e. 'hamburger', 'tea') and the intonation:

I'd like a hamburger, please.

Could I have a cup of tea, please?

5 Fluency Practice

a Divide the class into pairs and explain that they have to ask for things and reply. One student will ask and choose from the first list and the other will reply using the second list. Make sure that they take turns at this.

2 Model Phrases

Asking

I'll have a Coke, please.
Can I have a green salad, please.
I'd like some coffee, please.
Could I have a cup of tea, please.
Could you pass (me) the salt, please.

Response

Yes, of course.
Yes, certainly.
Here you are.

3 Notes

a 'Could you pass (me)' is used when you want someone near you to give you something, e.g.:

Could you pass me the potatoes, please?
Could you pass the ashtray, please?
Could you pass the salt, please?

b 'Here you are/Here it is' is used when you give something to someone.

4 Pronunciation

Now listen carefully and repeat.

5 Fluency Practice Exercises

a With a partner use this table to make short dialogues asking for things. One will ask and the other will reply.

Asking			Response
I'd like Could I have Could you pass me I'll have Can I have	some bread a cup of tea some fish and chips an apple a glass of orange juice some cheese a piece of cake some butter a chicken sandwich a cup of coffee a glass of lemonade some potatoes	please.	Yes, certainly. Yes, of course. Here you are. Here it is.

b Divide the students into pairs and explain that they are in a restaurant. Discuss the items on the menu and find out if any of the students have eaten in a British restaurant. Explain any unfamiliar vocabulary. Tell the students to take the part of the waiter/waitress or the customer and point out that the questions for the waiter/waitress are written on the left. The customer must respond to the questions by ordering things from the menu. When they have finished tell them to change roles and the customer must order different things.

b Restaurant Practice

Use this menu to practise ordering in a restaurant. Work in pairs and take it in turns to be the waiter/waitress and the customer. Use the information on the menu to answer the questions.

Waiter/Waitress   **Customer**

Would you like to
order now?

CLIFTON RESTAURANT

What would you like
to start with?

Starters:
soup
melon
fruit juice

What about the
main course?

Main course:
roast beef
grilled chicken
lamb chops
fried plaice

Which vegetables
would you like?

Vegetables:
potatoes, carrots
beans, peas

And anything for
dessert?

Dessert:
apple pie and cream
fruit salad
cheese and biscuits

What would you
like to drink?

Drinks:

soft drinks
orange juice, coke

wine:
red, white

coffee
tea

6 Further Practice

Explain that this is a menu for a small snack bar and go over any unfamiliar vocabulary. Divide the class into pairs and tell them to take the part of the waiter/waitress and customer as above and order things from the menu. Tell them to refer to the questions in Part 5a for the waiter/waitress if they need help. This could also be done as a group exercise with several students as customers and one as the waiter/waitress.

7 Situations

Please refer to the Introduction (page 7).

Suggested Answers

a Could I have the speciality of the house, please?
b I'd like a glass of red wine, please.
c Could you pass (me) the pepper, please?
d Could I have a cup of tea and some biscuits, please?
e I'd like a chicken salad, please.
f Can I have a black coffee, please?
g I'd like a packet of crisps, please.
h Can you pass (me) the sugar, please?
i Could I have a glass of water, please?
j I'll have a cup of white coffee, please.

6 Further Practice

In pairs use this menu to order a meal in a snack bar. One person will be the customer and the other will be the waiter/waitress, and then change around. Use these phrases to help you, as in Exercise 5b, e.g. 'What would you like?' 'What about ...?' 'Would you like ...?'

Sam's Snack Bar

sandwiches		**sweets**	
beef	tuna	ice cream (vanilla, strawberry,	
ham	tomato	chocolate, peppermint)	
cheese	chicken	apple pie	
egg	salmon	chocolate cake	

salads		**drinks**	
mixed	chicken	coffee	milk
green	beef	tea	Coke, Pepsi
tomato	egg and cheese	mineral water	
rice	corn and pepper	juice (orange, apple, tomato,	
		grapefruit)	

soup	
chicken	mushroom
tomato	celery
minestrone	onion

7 Situations

a You are in a restaurant and you want the speciality of the house. What do you say?

b In a bar a friend asks you what you would like to drink. What do you reply?

c During dinner with friends you want the pepper which is at the other side of the table. What do you say?

d You want a cup of tea and some biscuits in a café. What do you say to the waitress?

e You are in a snack bar with a friend who asks what you would like to have for lunch. How do you reply?

f You are standing at the drinks machine in your company/school and a colleague asks what you want. What do you say?

g You are at a kiosk and want to buy something because you're a bit hungry. What do you ask for?

h You are sitting at a table in your company/school cafeteria and you want the sugar which is on the next table. What do you say?

i You are at a friend's house and are very thirsty. What do you ask for?

j You are in the middle of a long meeting and the secretary comes to ask if you want a snack or a drink. What do you say?

Asking for Things
Part B   Shops and Services

1 Presentation

a Follow the procedure outlined in the Introduction (page 4) about relevant expressions. Explain to the class that Part B is about asking for things in shops and asking for services. Give the students any unfamiliar vocabulary from the table which is in three columns as in Unit 6 Part A (see p. 61). Tell the class they will hear eight short dialogues in which people are asking for things.

b Do the controlled oral practice exercise in the same way as for Unit 6 Part A (see p. 60).

Asking for Things
Part B Shops and Services

Presentation

a Listen to the tape and fill in the spaces:

	Asking Phrases	What	Reply
i	May I have And could I have	a dozen eggs, please? some cheese, please?	Of course. Here you are. I'm sorry but we've run out of cheese.
ii	Have you got	an English dictionary?	Yes, what sort would you like?
iii	I'd like	some grey shoes, please.	Yes, what size do you want?
iv	Could I have And I want to send	five stamps for letters to Saudi Arabia, please? two postcards to France.	Mmm … anything else? Certainly, here you are.
v	Hello, I'd like to change	these travellers' cheques, please.	Certainly.
vi	Have you got	a local newspaper please?	No, I'm afraid I haven't.
vii	Have you got	any batteries for clocks, please?	I'm sorry but we haven't.
viii	I'd like	a long woollen scarf, please.	Certainly. What colour?

b In pairs repeat these short dialogues. One will ask and the other will reply, and then change around.

2 Model Phrases

Follow the procedure outlined in the Introduction (page 5) about model phrases. When discussing the model phrases it would be a good idea to introduce the vocabulary related to shops in addition to the use of the phrases. Go over quantity words such as 'a few', 'several', 'half a dozen', 'a pair', 'some', 'a lot', as well as the question words 'how much/many'. Go over the vocabulary for size, shapes and weights such as 'a kilo', 'a pound', 'large/medium/small', 'width/height/length' as well as colours and containers such as 'box/carton/tube/bag/tin'.

3 Notes

Please refer to the Introduction (page 5).

4 Pronunciation

Points to note are:

a The emphasis is on the thing you are asking for, e.g.:

Have you got any blue shirts?

Could I have a jar of coffee, please.

b The pronunciation of some [səm] in the phrase

May I have some eggs, please.

c The contracted form 'I'd' [aɪd].

2 Model Phrases

Asking

> Could I have a tube of toothpaste, please?
> Can I have some apples, please?
> May I have a pair of red socks, please?
> I'd like some shampoo, please.
> Have you got any dark blue shoes?

Response

> Yes, certainly.
> Yes, of course.
> How many/much would you like?
> What size/colour/type do you want?
> No, I'm afraid I haven't.
> No, I'm sorry but we've run out of them.
> No, I'm sorry I haven't.

Specifications

> I'd like two/half a dozen/a kilo/a bag/three cartons/
> a couple of packets/four tins.
> Have you got it in light green/pink/brown and beige checks/
> a flowered pattern/blue and white stripes?
> Small/medium/average/large size, please.

3 Notes

a In shops the assistant will often ask 'Can I help you?'.
b 'Have you got ...?' is only used in shops when you are not sure if they sell what you want.

4 Pronunciation

Now listen carefully and repeat.

5 Fluency Practice Exercises

a Divide the class into pairs and explain that they have to imagine they are in a shop or post office and are customer and assistant respectively. One student has to ask for something by making a sentence and the other has to reply with an appropriate answer, taking it in turns. Ensure that sensible answers are given as not all of them are suitable and discuss alternatives with the class afterwards.

b This is a further pair work exercise with picture stimuli using the same situation as above. The phrases used by the shop assistant are standard language for shops in Britain and should be explained beforehand. Use the example to show the students what to do and allow a little time to study the pictures. Tell them to take turns at asking and answering and then discuss the alternative answers with the class afterwards.

5 Fluency Practice Exercises

a With a partner use this table to make short dialogues asking for things. One will ask and the other will reply.

Could I have May I have Can I have I'd like Have you got	a packet of envelopes a pair of black trousers some bread a packet of tea some apples three stamps for Brazil two 60-minute cassettes a postal order a box of tennis balls a pair of woollen gloves a bicycle pump some batteries for a digital watch	please?

Response

Yes, certainly.
Yes, of course.
I'm afraid we haven't got any.
What colour/size/type would you like?
How much/many do you want?
I'm sorry but we've run out (of it/them).
I'm sorry but I haven't.

b Work in pairs. One student (A) will be the shop assistant and the other student (B) will be the customer. Look at the pictures to help you. The first one is done for you.

i A: Can I help you?

B: I'd like some shampoo, please.

ii A: What would you like?

B: _____

6 Further Practice

Tell each student to prepare their four different shopping lists.
Following the same pattern of customer and assistant divide the students
into pairs and tell them to ask for the things on their lists and reply
accordingly and to take turns doing the parts. Monitor carefully for
pronunciation and accuracy and where possible record the exercises on
tape or on video and go over them later with the class.

ii A: Next, please

B: _____

iv A: Can I help you?

B: _____

v A: What would you like?

B: _____

vi A: Who's next?

B: _____

6 Further Practice

Prepare a shopping list of three things you need at four different shops, e.g. Post Office, chemist's, butcher's, etc. Work in pairs taking it in turns to be the customer and the shopkeeper and ask for the things you want. Use the phrases in Exercise 5b to help you, e.g.:

A: Can I help you?
B: Yes, please, I'd like ...

7 Situations

Please refer to the Introduction (page 7).

Suggested Answers

a Could I have a pair of sunglasses, please?
b How much is it to send two letters to Japan?
c Could I cash these travellers' cheques, please?
d I'd like (to look at) a blue and white striped shirt, please.
e I'd like (a copy of) *Star Wars III*, please.
f I'd like some white A5 paper and a dozen envelopes, please.
g Have you got the latest issue of *Computer World*?
h I'd like to send this parcel to New York, please.
i Could you tell me the exchange rate for dollars, please?
j I'd like a bottle of shampoo for dry hair and a tube of mint toothpaste, please.
k I'd like a blue woollen scarf, please.
l Could I have three C-60 cassettes and the latest hit by Zodiac Mindwarp, please?

7 Situations

a You want a new pair of sunglasses. What do you say in the shop?

b You want to send two letters to Japan. Ask for the stamps in the Post Office.

c You want to cash some travellers' cheques at the bank. What do you say?

d You want to buy some new shirts. Ask the assistant for help.

e You want to buy the latest best seller by your favourite author. What do you say in the book store?

f You need some writing paper and envelopes. What do you say in the shop?

g At the newsagent's you want a magazine about computers/fashion/photography/cooking. What do you say?

h You want to send a heavy parcel of books to New York. What do you say at the Post Office?

i At the bank you want to find out the exchange rate for dollars. What do you ask?

j At the chemist's you need a tube of toothpaste and a bottle of shampoo. What do you say?

k It's very cold and snowing so you want to buy a warm scarf. What do you ask for in the shop?

l You need some blank cassettes for recording and a record by your favourite singer. What do you say in the shop?

Revision Units 1 – 6

The first six units of the Student's Book are all covered in the exercises of this Revision Section. In some cases more than one of the newly acquired skills is used in an exercise, particularly where they are closely connected, e.g. Meetings and Introductions (Unit 1) and Talking about Yourself (Unit 2). This section can be used after the first six units have been completed or referred to when the class are at a later stage in the book but need to go over the material again.

Exercise 1

a At a Party

Explain to the students that they are at a party and choose one student as the host/hostess. Tell them to study the information on the example card about Charlie Brown and then give each student a card. Explain that they have to make up some similar information about a different imaginary person, giving name, age, job, interests, etc. and write it on the card. Before beginning the role play exercise explain that they have to mix with the host/hostess and other guests at the 'party' and they should introduce themselves and talk to the others. Remind the students to use the phrases from Unit 1 (Meetings and Introductions) and Unit 2 (Talking about Yourself) and if necessary briefly revise the material before they begin the exercise. In the case of a large class they could be divided into smaller groups. Go round the groups/class noting any mistakes to check at the end.

b At a Conference

This exercise is an extension of the previous one and is useful for classes with business, technical and professional students who may have to go to conferences. Explain the situation and then give out a card to each student as above. Divide the class into government representatives and businessmen/women and tell them to invent the necessary details for their cards which should be prepared as in Part a of this exercise using the example in the book. Do the exercise in the same way as Part a.

Revision Units 1 – 6

Unit 1   Meetings and Introductions
Unit 2   Talking about Yourself
Unit 3   Giving Yourself Time to Think
Unit 4   Not Understanding
Unit 5   Asking for and Giving Information
Unit 6   Asking for Things

1 a Imagine you are at a party and the rest of the class are guests. Choose one person to be the host/hostess and then introduce yourself to the other people at the party and talk about yourself.

Look at this information about a man called Charlie Brown.

> ## Charlie Brown
>
> age 25 — single
> sports — swimming, skiing, sailing
> interests — cooking, collecting stamps
> job — stockbroker
> lives in London

Make up a card like it with similar information about another man or woman and use it to talk about yourself at the party. Remember to use the phrases in Unit 1 for meetings and introductions and the phrases from Unit 2 for talking about yourself.

b Imagine you are at an international conference in New York about Social Problems in Business and Industry. You are a representative of your company or your government and you must introduce yourself to the other delegates at the conference. Work in small groups.

Prepare a card with details about a suitable job like this example and use your card to talk about yourself at the conference.

> ## Arthur Carruthers
>
> age 45
> married, 3 children (15, 12, 8)
>   and 2 dogs, 3 cats
> sports — golf, jogging, tennis
> hobbies — collecting antique clocks
> job — economist
> lives in New York

Use the phrases from Unit 1 for meetings and introductions and the phrases from Unit 2 for talking about your job and also Unit 4 if you don't understand.

Exercise 2

This exercise revises Asking for and Giving Information, including directions (Unit 5) and also Giving Time to Think (Unit 3). Divide the class into pairs and explain that one has to ask for directions to the places marked on the map and the other has to give them. Allow time for them to study the map and tell them to take turns at asking and replying. If time allows tell the class to mark a few more places on the map for extra practice. Remind the students to give themselves time to think where they need to work out the answer.

Exercise 3

These exercises are intended to revise Asking for Things (Unit 6) although as in the other cases additional units may be incidentally covered, e.g. Not Understanding (Unit 4).

a Shopping

Tell the class to draw up a shopping list of items they require in the various places and explain any lexis they don't understand. (Depending on the level of the class the teacher can decide how many shops and how many items for each one.) Elicit from the students a few items that could be found in each of the places and write them on the board. Divide the class into pairs and explain that they should take it in turns to act as assistant or customer. Where necessary briefly revise the phrases in Unit 6, Part B and discuss how to use them. Refer the students to Unit 6, Part B, exercise 5a and b in the Student's Book (page 37).

2 Working in pairs use the map to ask for and give directions to the places marked. You are standing at X.

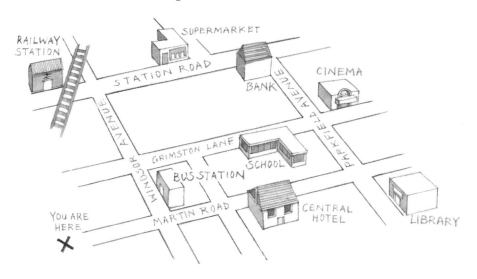

Use the phrases in Unit 3 to give yourself time to think before you answer and use the phrases in Unit 5 for directions.

3 **a** Make shopping lists of things you want:

    i In the supermarket.
    ii At the Post Office.
    iii In the department store.
    iv At the chemist's.
    v At the newsagent's.

Here are some examples to help you. Work in pairs with one student as the customer and the other as the shopkeeper or shop assistant.

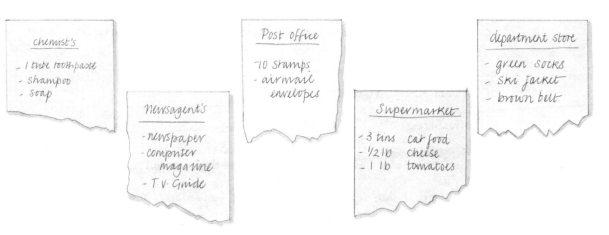

Now add some more things to the lists if you want. Remember to use the phrases in Unit 6 for asking for things and the phrases in Unit 4 if you don't understand.

b In a Restaurant

Explain that the class should make up menus with suitable dishes and drinks. Discuss briefly the sort of things they could include (either from their own country or another, e.g. Britain) and write a sample menu on the board if there are any problems with vocabulary. Divide the class into pairs or small groups and if required arrange the classroom like a restaurant with one student acting as the waiter/waitress and the other(s) as customer(s). The customers can order from the menu while the waiter/waitress takes the order. Refer the students to Unit 6, Part A, exercise 5b in the Student's Book (page 33).

Exercise 4

This exercise revises Giving Time to Think (Unit 3) as well as Not Understanding (Unit 4) and Asking for and Giving Information (Unit 5).

Divide the class into two teams (or more if the class is large) and tell them to make up a General Knowledge Quiz of about twenty to thirty questions. The Student's Book has several suggestions under category titles although students should be encouraged to think of their own categories. When the teams are ready check their questions for accuracy and seat the teams facing each other (if there are two teams) or in different parts of the classroom if there are more. If necessary choose one student (or the teacher) to keep the score and tell the team members to ask the other team the questions in turn. If possible record or video the activity to check for mistakes afterwards.

Exercise 5

This exercise practises all the first six units of the book. There are four consecutive dialogues about a man's first day at a new job. The students have to make up the dialogue using the information given in the book. This could be done as a written exercise for homework first and then practised in class or orally as a pair work exercise and then 'performed' for the rest of the class. There are several possible alternatives for the dialogues.

Exercise 5 Sample Answers

i In the Street

A: Excuse me, can you tell me where Compuco is, please?
B: Um ... just a moment. Yes, go straight and then turn left. It's on the right.
A: I'm sorry, I didn't quite catch that. Could you repeat it, please?
B: (Slowly) Yes, go straight and then turn left, it's on the right.
A: Thank you very much.

b Look at page 33 (Unit 6 Part A) and prepare a similar menu with dishes from your country. Working in pairs or small groups use the menu to order in a restaurant. One will be the waiter/waitress and the other(s) will be the customer(s). Use the phrases in Unit 6 for asking for things to help you.

4 Divide into two teams and make a general knowledge quiz for the other team. Ask and answer the questions in turn and use the phrases from Unit 3 for giving yourself time to think and Unit 4 for not understanding if necessary. Also, use the phrases from Unit 5 for asking for and giving information.

Here are some examples to help. You can ask questions about the geography or history of your country or other countries, about books, films, music and television programmes, about science and technology or about current events and famous people.

History and Geography:
  What's the highest mountain in the world?
  Where is the longest river in the world?

Books, Films, Music and Television Programmes:
  Who wrote a famous Ninth Symphony?
  What popular American TV programme is located in Texas?

Science and Technology:
  When was the first landing on the Moon?
  Where can you find microprocessors?

Current Events and Famous People:
  How many countries are there in the European Community?
  What's the name of the Queen in Britain?

5 In pairs prepare these dialogues. You are going to a new job on the first day.

  i In the Street:
    A: You are looking for Compuco Company and you ask a stranger in the street.
    B: You need time to think. Then answer and give the directions.
    A: You don't hear very well. Ask him/her to tell you again.
    B: You repeat the directions.
    A: You thank him/her.

ii In the Office

A: Hello.

B: Hello, I'm Anne Jones.

A: Nice to meet you. I'm Bill Winter.

B: Where are you from?

A: I'm from London. What about you?

B: I'm from Bristol. I work in the Export Department.

A: Could you tell me the office hours and break times?

B: Yes, from 9 to 5 with one hour for lunch at 1 o'clock. There's a coffee break in the morning for twenty minutes around 10.30 and another in the afternoon about 3.30.

A: Could you tell me where the canteen is?

B: Yes, it's on this floor. Go down the corridor to the end and turn right.

A: Um . . . down to the end, and turn right. Thanks. Bye.

B: Not at all. Bye.

ii In the Office:

A: You see another employee and say hello.

B: You introduce yourself to the new employee.

A: You answer.

B: You ask him where he's from.

A: You reply and ask her the same question.

B: You reply and tell him which department you are in.

A: You want to know about the office hours and break times. Ask.

B: You give the information.

A: You want to know where the canteen is. Ask.

B: You give the directions.

A: You repeat the directions. Then thank her.

B: You reply.

iii During Lunch in the Canteen

A: Could you pass (me) the salt, please?
B: Yes, of course. Here you are.
A: Thank you.
B: Not at all.
A: Excuse me, do you know where I can get a cup of coffee?
B: Yes, over there by the door.
A: Thanks. Can you tell me if it's possible to get weekly tickets or vouchers for the canteen?
B: Yes, it is. You can get them from the canteen manager.
A: Thanks. I must get back to work now. Bye.
B: Bye.

iii During Lunch in the Canteen:
    A: You want the salt. Ask the person next to you.
    B: You pass it.
    A: You thank him/her.
    B: You reply.
    A: You want a cup of coffee. Ask the person at your table where you can get it.
    B: You reply.
    A: You thank him/her.
    B: You reply.
    A: You want to know if it is possible to get weekly tickets or·vouchers for the canteen. Ask the person beside you.
    B: You reply.
    A: You thank him/her and leave the table.
    B: You reply.

iv In the Office Supplies Department

B: Can I help you?

A: Yes, I need some pens and pencils for my desk.

B: How many do you need and what type?

A: Oh ... about half a dozen of the blue pencils and several ball point pens in different colours.

B: Pardon. Could you repeat that, please?

A: I said six blue pencils and several ball point pens in different colours.

B: Here you are.

A: Thanks very much.

B: Do you need anything else?

A: Could I have some paper clips ... and, let me see ... some notepads, please.

B: What size paper clips do you want?

A: Er ... now, let me think ... large, please.

B: And what about the notepads ... how many ... what kind?

A: Two or three ... medium size, please.

B: Here they are.

A: Thanks a lot.

B: By the way, I'm Miss Scroogle, the Head of the Stationery Department.

A: Nice to meet you ... I'm Anne Winter ... I must go now ... bye.

iv In the Office Supplies Department:
   B: You ask if you can help.
   A: You explain that you need some pens and pencils for your desk.
   B: You ask how many and what type he wants.
   A: You reply.
   B: You don't hear clearly. Ask him to repeat.
   A: Repeat.
   B: You give him the supplies.
   A: You thank him/her.
   B: You ask if he needs anything else.
   A: You want some paper clips and some notepads. Ask for them.
   B: You ask about the size of the paper clips.
   A: You aren't sure. Hesitate before you reply.
   B: You ask about which type of notepads and how many.
   A: You reply.
   B: You give him the supplies.
   A: You thank him/her.
   B: You introduce yourself.
   A: You reply. Then you leave and return to your office.

Unit 7   Making Offers, Accepting and Refusir

Students of English always need to know what to say when offering things such as cigarettes, cups of coffee, etc. as well as how to accept or refuse them politely. Similarly, they also need to know what to say when they offer to do something or to perform a small service for another person. This unit aims to equip the student with the necessary phrases for this function.

See Introduction for instructions on how to use each exercise.

1 Presentation

a Follow the procedure outlined in the Introduction (page 4) about relevant expressions. Pre-teach any unknown vocabulary such as 'fruit juice', 'suitcase', etc. Explain to the class that they will hear eight short dialogues in which people offer things or offer to do things for another person and that they have to complete the table accordingly.

b Divide the students into pairs for the controlled oral practice. Using the table as a model, one student has to make the offer and the other has to accept or refuse accordingly. If necessary do one or two together first as an example and ensure that the students in each pair take it in turns to offer and respond.

Unit 7

Making Offers, Accepting and Refusing

Presentation

a Listen to the tape and fill in the spaces:

	Offer	Accept	Refuse
i	Would you like a Coke?	Yes please, I'd love one.	
ii	Would you like a cup of coffee?		No, thanks, not just at the moment.
iii	How about some pudding?	Yes, please, I'd love some.	
iv	Can I get you a sandwich?	That's very kind of you, thanks.	
v	Let me help you with that heavy suitcase.		Thanks, but it's all right.
vi	How about a piece of chocolate cake?	Yes, please, I'd love one.	
vii	Can I help with the dishes?		No, thank you, I can manage.
viii	Would you like some biscuits?		No, thanks, not right now.

2 Model Phrases

Follow the procedure outlined in the Introduction (page 5) about model phrases. Point out carefully the differences between offering a thing (e.g. 'Would you like/How about?') and offering to do something ('Let me help you/Can I do it?') and the relevant answers for acceptance and refusal as given in the table.

3 Notes

a Point out that the way to answer an offer with 'a' or 'an' in it is to use the word 'one'. Practise with further examples to clarify the construction,
   e.g. Would you like **a** Coke?   Yes, please, I'd love **one**.

b It is not necessary to repeat the thing being offered; in fact, it sounds strange and unnatural.

c/d Stress the difference between the phrases used for offering something and offering to do something. They are not the same thing and cannot be interchanged.

b Work in pairs and practise these dialogues. One will offer and the other will accept or refuse and then change around.

2 Model Phrases

Offers

Would you like a cup of tea? / something to eat?

How about some biscuits? / a coffee?

Let me help you with your bag.
Can I do it?

Accepting

Yes, please, I'd love one. / some.

That's very kind / good of you, thanks.

Thank you, that's very kind.

Refusing

No, thanks, I can manage. / it's all right.

Not for me, thanks.

No, thanks, not right now. / at the moment.

No, thank you.

3 Notes

a Notice the answers to 'a/an/some':

	Response
Would you like a glass of juice?	Yes, please, I'd love one.
How about an apple?	Yes, please, I'd love one.
Would you like some fruit?	Yes, please, I'd love some.

b Do not repeat the noun in the answer:

	Response
Would you like a cup of tea?	Yes, please, I'd love one. (*Not* I'd love a cup of tea)
How about some more biscuits?	Yes, please, I'd love some. (*Not* I'd love some biscuits)

c For offering something (Would you like/how about?):
  Would you like my newspaper?
  How about some biscuits?

d For offering to do something (Can I/let me.):
  Can I pass you the salt?
  Let me carry that suitcase for you.
  Let me help with the washing up.

4 Pronunciation

Points to note in the exercise are:

a The emphasis is on the thing being offered, e.g.:

Would you like a cup of tea?

How about some cake?

b Notice the stress on 'love' and 'very kind':

I'd love one.

That's very kind of you.

c Notice the slight fall in intonation:

No, thanks.

No, thank you.

5 Fluency Practice Exercises

a Divide the class into pairs and explain that one has to ask and the other has to answer. Point out that there may be several possible answers to a question although some are quite impossible. Here it is essential for the students to have understood the importance of offering a thing or offering to do something for somebody. Ensure that they ask and answer in turns and afterwards go through the various possible answers all together.

b Divide the class into pairs and explain that one student has to offer and then the other has to accept or refuse according to the picture (X = refuse). Point out that the phrase for making the offer is already given and allow time to look at the pictures. Tell one pair to read for all the class to hear so as to establish the pattern correctly and then tell the students to do the example again in their pairs. Tell them to take it in turns to ask and respond and when they have finished discuss the possible alternative answers.

4 Pronunciation

Now listen carefully and repeat.

5 Fluency Practice Exercises

a With a partner match the offers and the answers. Some offers may
have several possible answers.

Would you like some milk?	No, thanks, it's all right, I can manage.
Would you like a drink?	Yes, please, I'd love one.
How about a cigarette?	Oh, thank you. I'll have a lemonade.
Can I pass you those books?	Yes, please. I'll have a Coke.
Let me get you a chair.	That's very kind of you.
Can I help you with that box?	No, thanks, not just at the moment.
How about some biscuits?	Yes, please, I'd love some.
Let me open that bottle for you.	Thanks very much.
Would you like my umbrella?	Not for me, thanks.
How about a chocolate?	No, thanks, I can manage.

b Work in pairs for this exercise. One student will offer and the other
will accept or refuse according to the picture. (X across the picture =
refuse.) We have done the first one for you.

i A: Would you like a glass of milk?   ii A: Would you like a cigarette?

B: Yes, please. I'd love one.   B: _____

6 Further Practice

Elicit from the students the kinds of things that somebody might win as prizes in a competition, e.g. cars, washing machines, holidays, watches, computers, etc., and discuss with them what they would choose. Divide the students into pairs and explain that one has just won a competition and can choose three prizes in a TV game. Each student in turn has to be the organiser of the competition and has to think of at least six possible prizes to offer his/her partner. The organiser then has to offer the prizes to the winner who can accept three but must refuse three. When they have finished discuss the various offers all together.

7 Situations

Please refer to the Introduction (page 7).

Suggested Answers

a Would you like a drink?
b No, thanks, I don't smoke.
c That's very kind of you, thanks.
d Let me pass you the bread.
e Can I collect your book from the library?
f No, thanks, I can manage.
g Thanks very much, that's very good of you.
h Let me open the window.
i Can I pass the sandwiches?
j That's very kind, thank you.

iii A: _____   iv A: _____

B: _____   B: _____

v A: _____   vi A: _____

B: _____   B: _____

6 Further Practice

Work in pairs. One student has just won some prizes in a TV
competition; the organiser of the TV competition will offer six prizes,
and the contestant must accept three and refuse three.
e.g.:

A: Would you like a holiday for two in New York?

B: Yes, please, I'd love one.

7 Situations

a Offer a drink to someone.
b Someone offers you a cigarette. Refuse.
c A friend offers you a lift to the station. Accept.
d Offer to pass the bread at dinner.
e Offer to collect a friend's book from the library.
f Someone offers to carry your shopping. Refuse.
g A friend offers to lend you some cassettes for a party. Accept.
h Offer to open the window.
i Offer to pass the sandwiches at a party.
j Someone offers to lend you a pen. Accept.

Unit 8   Invitations

To be able to issue invitations and to know how to accept or refuse them is one of the most important functions in any language. In their social or professional lives students of English will probably want to ask people to go to places with them or will need to know how to respond appropriately when they themselves are being invited. This unit aims to equip students with the necessary language to do this confidently.

See Introduction for instructions on how to use each exercise.

1 Presentation

a Follow the procedure outlined in the Introduction (page 4) about relevant expressions. Discuss with students the kinds of places they would invite English speaking friends to visit in their home towns and how they would do so. Then explain that they will hear seven short dialogues in which people are invited to go to various places or to do various things and explain any unfamiliar vocabulary. In the table there are three columns – in the first there are the words used for the actual invitation, in the second there is the day and time and in the third there is the response of the person being invited.

b Divide the class into pairs for the controlled oral exercise. Tell them to use the table to invite and respond accordingly and ensure that they take turns at this.

Unit 8

Invitations

Presentation

a Listen to the tape and fill in the spaces:

	Invitation	Day/time	Yes/no
i	Would you like to <u>go out</u> for <u>dinner</u>	on <u>Friday</u>, Anne?	That's <u>very kind</u> of you, Tom. I'd <u>love to</u>.
ii	Are you free to <u>come</u> to the disco <u>with me</u>	<u>tonight</u>, Jane?	Yes, <u>please</u>. I'd <u>love to</u>.
iii	<u>Would you like</u> to <u>come</u> to my party	on <u>Saturday</u> evening?	That's very <u>kind of you</u> but I'm afraid <u>I can't</u>.
iv	<u>Do you want</u> to come to London with us	at <u>the weekend</u>?	Thanks <u>for asking me</u> but I'm <u>afraid I</u> can't.
v	<u>Would you like to</u> play tennis	<u>this afternoon</u>?	That would be <u>very nice</u>, I'd <u>love to</u>.
vi	<u>Are you free to</u> come for a picnic	<u>on</u> Saturday <u>afternoon</u>?	Thanks for the invitation but <u>I'm afraid I</u> can't.
vii	Would you <u>like to</u> see the new art exhibition	after work <u>tomorrow</u>?	Yes, <u>I'd love to</u>.

2 Model Phrases

Follow the procedure outlined in the Introduction (page 5) about model phrases. Notice carefully the different ways of inviting and the phrases used for accepting or refusing. Notice too that even when refusing you thank the person for inviting you or say how much you would like to accept although it is impossible. Refer to the Presentation exercise (where the students suggested places they would invite English speaking friends to go) and begin practising the model phrases by using the places the students mentioned.

3 Notes

a Point out that the place or activity mentioned in the invitation is not repeated in the response as it sounds strange and artificial.

b Explain that the phrase 'I'm afraid' is often used in English to say 'I'm sorry' at the beginning of an excuse.

4 Pronunciation

Points to note:

a The rising intonation in:

Would you like to come to dinner?

Would you like to go to the cinema?

Would you like to play tennis?

The word 'kind' is stressed in the phrase:

That's very kind of you.

b The contracted form 'I'd' [aɪd] and the stress and intonation in the phrase:

I'd love to.

c The words 'sorry' and 'can't' are stressed in the phrase:

I'm sorry but I can't,

and 'asking' and 'can't' in the phrase:

Thanks for asking me but I can't.

d The word 'busy' is stressed and note the pronunciation of 'then' [ðen]:

I'm afraid I'm busy then.

b Work in pairs and practise these dialogues. One will invite and the other will refuse. Take turns at this.

2 Model phrases

Inviting

Would you like to	go to the museum this afternoon? come to dinner on Saturday?
Are you free to	play tennis on Wednesday? go to the cinema tomorrow?
Do you want to	go to the concert tomorrow evening? come to lunch next weekend?

Accepting

That's very kind of you.
That would be very nice.
Yes, please. I'd love to.

Refusing

I'd love to but I'm afraid I can't.
Thanks for asking me but I'm sorry I can't.
Thanks for the invitation but I'm busy then.

3 Notes

a Do not repeat the verb in your answer, e.g.:

Response

Would you like to Do you want to	come to lunch?	Yes, please, I'd love to. (*Not* I'd love to come to lunch.)
Are you free to come out tonight?		That's very kind of you but I'm afraid I can't. (*Not* I can't come out.)

b 'I'm afraid' = 'I'm sorry', e.g.:

I'm afraid
I'm sorry } I can't go to the party.

4 Pronunciation

Now listen carefully and repeat.

5 Fluency Practice Exercises

a Divide the class into pairs and explain that one of them has to invite
while the other accepts or refuses, taking it in turns to do so. There are
many combinations which can be used in any order, and in fact all
answers are possible.

b Divide the students into pairs and tell them to take turns at inviting
and accepting or refusing. Follow the same procedure as in Unit 7,
Exercise 5b (see p. 94). Note that after question (i) only some of the
words are given as prompts, not the whole invitation.

5 Fluency Practice Exercises

a With a partner use this table to make dialogues for invitations. One person will give the invitation and the other will accept or refuse. Take turns at this.

Invitation

Would you like Are you free Do you want	to go swimming to go dancing to go to the theatre to play tennis to go for a walk to come for dinner to visit the exhibition to go to the football match to come to a party to have lunch with us to play golf to see the new art exhibition to go to a concert	tomorrow? on Friday evening? after work? this evening? on Saturday? on the 23rd? next weekend? on Thursday? next Sunday?

Response

Yes, please That's very kind of you	I'd love to.
Thanks for the invitation That would be very nice Thanks for asking me	but I can't. but I'm sorry I'm busy.

b Look at the pictures and working in pairs take it in turns to make the invitations and accept or refuse. (X across the picture = refuse.) We have done the first one for you.

i A: Would you like to go to the cinema tonight?

ii A: .... next Friday?

iii A: .... this afternoon?

B: That's very kind of you. I'd love to.

B: _____

B: _____

6 Further Practice

Before beginning the exercise discuss with the class the arrangements you would need to make for a party such as date, time, place, etc. and the questions people invited might ask, e.g. 'What time does it start?' 'What can I bring?'. Divide the students into pairs and tell them they are the parents/friends of another student of their own choice in the class. Tell each pair to work out the necessary details for a surprise birthday party. When they are all ready tell the students to go round inviting the others to come and they will accept or refuse. Encourage the students who are the guests to ask for more information if they accept by asking such questions as 'What sort of present shall I buy?' or 'Shall I bring something to drink?'.

7 Situations

Please refer to the Introduction (page 7).

Suggested Answers

a I'd love to come but I'm busy on Friday.
b Would you like to go to the cinema on Saturday evening?
c Do you want to play squash on Tuesday or Wednesday evening?
d That's very kind of you, I'd love to.
e Are you free to have a drink in a café now?
f Thanks for asking me but I'm afraid I can't.
g Do you want to go for a walk?

v A: .... Saturday
       morning?

B: _____

v A: .... at the weekend?

B: _____

vi A: .... after work?

B: _____

6 Further Practice

Working in pairs imagine you are the parents/friends of another student and you are planning a surprise birthday party for him/her. Work out the time, place and other details and then go around to the other pairs and invite them to come to the party. They will accept or refuse your invitation.

7 Situations

a A colleague invites you for dinner on Friday evening but you are busy that night.

b You want to invite a friend to go to the cinema at the weekend. What will you say?

c At the Sports Centre you want to invite a friend to play squash with you next week. What will you say?

d Your boss asks you to have lunch on Monday. What will you say?

e You see some friends you met on holiday last summer and you want to invite them to have a drink in a café. What will you say?

f You are invited to a big party next weekend but you are going away. What will you say?

g It's a nice sunny day and you want to go for a walk. Telephone a colleague and invite him/her to go with you.

Unit 9   Asking for Permission

In everyday social intercourse politeness often demands that we ask others for permission to do things, e.g. open a window, smoke a cigarette and so on; also, in some cases we must give or refuse permission. This unit aims to answer that need for the student of English.

See Introduction for instructions on how to use each exercise.

1 Presentation

a Follow the procedure outlined in the Introduction (page 4) about relevant expressions. Briefly discuss with the students the kind of situation in which they would need to ask for permission to do things and also ask them which ones they would agree to and which they would refuse. Before playing the cassette explain any unfamiliar vocabulary. Then tell the students that they will hear nine short dialogues in which people ask for permission to do various things and that permission is either given or not in the responses. Explain that in the table the first column is for asking, the second one is for what they want to do and the third one for the agreeing or refusing phrases.

b Divide the students into pairs for the controlled oral practice exercise and tell them to use the table to ask for permission and then accept or refuse as given. Make sure that they take turns at asking and answering.

Unit 9

Asking for Permission

Presentation

Listen to the tape and fill in the spaces:

	Asking	What	Yes/no
i	Is it all right	if I close the window?	Yes, of course.
ii	Is it possible for me	to use your telephone?	No, I'm afraid you can't. It's out of order.
iii	Could I	borrow your pen?	By all means.
iv	Would it be possible	for me to arrive late for work tomorrow, Mr Parker?	I'm sorry but you can't. That would be the second time this week.
v	Do you think I could	turn off the radio?	Certainly, please do.
vi	Is it all right	if I smoke?	I'd rather you didn't.
vii	Could I	sit here?	I'm sorry but this seat is taken.
viii	May I	leave early this afternoon?	Yes, that's all right.
ix	Can I	switch on the light? It's a bit dark.	Yes, of course. Go ahead.

2 Model Phrases

Follow the procedure outlined in the Introduction (page 5) about model phrases.

3 Notes

a Point out that the action or activity mentioned in the request is not repeated in the answer as it sounds strange and artificial.

b Stress the use of the past tense after 'I'd rather' because it is important for the class to get it right at this stage. Make sure they realise that 'I'd' is the contraction of 'I would' and not 'I had', and encourage them to use the contracted form.

c Point out the use of the indirect object 'for me', 'for us', etc.

Would it be all right possible	+ for	me/us you him/her/them	+ to	go have borrow

d In English it sounds rude and abrupt to refuse a request without explanation and so a reason should be given for saying 'no'.

b Work in pairs and practise these dialogues. One will ask for permission and the other will agree or refuse accordingly. Take turns at it.

2 Model Phrases

Permission

Can I open the window?
Could I use your dictionary?
May I smoke?
Is it all right if I park here?
Would it be possible
    Is it possible for me to leave early?
Do you think I could borrow your lighter?

Yes

Yes, of course.
Yes, that's all right.
That's fine.
By all means.
Go ahead.
Certainly, please do.

No

No, I'm afraid you can't.
I'm sorry but ...
I'd rather you didn't.

3 Notes

a Do not repeat the action or activity in the answer:

	Response
Can I open the window?	Certainly, please do. (*Not* Please open it.)
Is it all right if I smoke?	Yes, of course. (*Not* Yes, of course you can smoke.)

b 'I'd rather + didn't':

Do you mind if I switch on the TV?	I'd rather you didn't. (*Not* I'd rather you don't.)
Could they arrive a bit late?	I'd rather they didn't. (*Not* I'd rather they don't.)

c 'Would it be all right for (someone) to (do something)?':

Would it be possible for me to leave early?
Is it all right for them to borrow the tapes?

d When refusing permission it is polite to give a reason:

May I borrow your pencil?	No, I'm afraid you can't. I need it myself.
Could I open the window?	I'd rather you didn't. I'm a bit cold.

4 Pronunciation

Points to note are:

a The short form of 'can' [kən] in 'Can I open the window?'

b The rising tone of the questions

Can I open the window? ↗

Is it all right if I use your phone? ↗

May I use your pen? ↗

Do you think I could smoke? ↗

with a slight emphasis on the words 'window', 'phone', 'pen', 'smoke'.

c The responses have a falling tone:

Yes, of course. ↘

That's quite all right. ↘

I'm afraid you can't. ↘

d The pronunciation of 'afraid' [əfreɪd] in the phrase:
I'm afraid you can't.

e The stress is on the word 'need' in the phrase:

I'm sorry but I need it.

5 Fluency Practice Exercises

a Divide the class into pairs and tell them to ask and respond in turns using the tables in their books. Explain that they have to work out appropriate questions as all the combinations are not possible. Practise one or two all together first to establish the pattern correctly.

b Divide the students into pairs and follow the same procedure as outlined in Unit 7, Exercise 5b (p. 94). Note that after question (i) only some words or none at all are given for the asking for permission phrase.

4 Pronunciation

Now listen carefully and repeat.

5 Fluency Practice Exercises

a With a partner ask for permission in these situations and then agree or refuse. Several alternatives are possible. Take turns at this.

Asking

May I	smoke	your umbrella?
Is it possible for me to	borrow	here?
Can I	sit	your radio?
Is it all right if I	use	in class?
Do you think I could	listen to	the newspaper?
Could I	have	the window?
Would it be possible for me to	close	another biscuit?

Response

Yes,	of course. that's all right. by all means. certainly. go ahead. please do.	No,	I'm afraid not. I'm sorry but... I'd rather you didn't. I'm afraid you can't.

b Work in pairs and look at the pictures. One student will ask for permission and the other will agree or refuse. (X across the picture = refuse.) We have done the first one for you.

A: Is it all right if I close the window?   ii A: ... smoke?   iii A: .... radio?

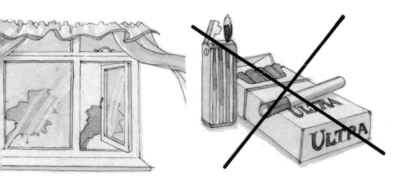

B: Certainly, please do.   B: _____   B: _____

6 Further Practice

Divide the students into pairs and tell them that one will ask for permission to do the things on the list and the other will agree or refuse. Where a student refuses a request tell him/her to think of a suitable reason for saying no. Tell the students to take turns at asking and responding.

7 Situations

Please refer to the Introduction (page 7).

Suggested Answers

a May I borrow your badminton racquet?
b Would it be possible for me to have a day off work tomorrow ... I want to visit my grandmother in hospital?
c I'd rather you didn't as I'm a bit cold.
d Is it all right if we sit here?
e Yes, of course ... by all means.
f Do you think I could bring a friend to dinner tomorrow?
g May I smoke?
h Could I turn on the light – it's a bit dark?
i Is it all right if I switch on the news?
j I'm sorry but I'm expecting a long distance call.
k Yes, of course.

iv A: .... borrow ....?   v A: .... use ....?   vi A: .... switch on ....?

B: _____   B: _____   B: _____

6 Further Practice

In pairs practise asking permission. One will ask to do these things and the other will accept or refuse according to the instructions. If you refuse try to think of a reason. Take it in turns.

a Have time off to go to the dentist. Refuse.
b Leave your car/bicycle in front of the house. Refuse.
c Change channels on the television. Refuse.
d Borrow some cassette tapes for a party. Accept.
e Arrive late for the next class. Refuse.
f Type a letter on your friend's typewriter. Accept.
g Switch off the heater. Refuse.
h Use a friend's telephone book. Accept.
i Close the curtains. Accept.

7 Situations

a Ask permission to borrow a badminton racquet.
b Ask permission to have a day off work tomorrow and give a reason.
c Somebody sitting opposite you in a train wants to open the window. Refuse and give a reason.
d Two people are sitting at a table in a café and there are two empty seats there. Ask if you and your friend can sit there.
e Somebody asks to borrow your book. Agree
f You are staying with an English family in England. Ask if you can bring a friend home to dinner.
g You are having dinner with friends and want to smoke at the table. Ask for permission.
h It's a bit dark in the room and you want to turn on the light. Ask for permission.
i You're visiting a friend and want to watch the news on TV. Ask for permission.
j Somebody asks to use your telephone. Refuse and give a reason.
k A friend wants to borrow some glasses for a party. Agree.

Unit 10 Likes and Dislikes

In everyday conversation people frequently discuss their likes and dislikes and this unit aims to enable students of English at this level to do this in a variety of different ways.

See Introduction for instructions on how to use each exercise.

1 Presentation

a Follow the procedure outlined in the Introduction (page 4) about relevant expressions. Discuss with the students their own personal likes and dislikes in music, films, fashion, etc. Explain any vocabulary in the exercise that may be unfamiliar such as 'old-fashioned', a 'Western' and so on. Tell the students that they will hear one conversation in which two people discuss various likes and dislikes in music and films. The students have to fill in the blank spaces in the usual way. Briefly compare and discuss the likes and dislikes expressed in the dialogue with the students' own preferences given at the start of the lesson.

b Divide the class into pairs and tell each pair to practise the dialogue, each taking a part in turn, and where time permits ask several pairs to act out the dialogue for the rest of the class.

Unit 10

Likes and Dislikes

1 Presentation

a Listen to the tape and fill in the spaces:

Jane:	Would you like to listen to some Beethoven?
Tom:	Yes, please. I <u>love</u> classical music.
Jane:	<u>So do I</u>. I like Beethoven <u>very</u> <u>much</u>. I'm <u>fond</u> <u>of</u> pop music, too.
Tom:	Are you? I'm <u>not</u>.
Jane:	Aren't you? Oh, I <u>love it</u>. I'm <u>very</u> <u>keen</u> on musical films, too.
Tom:	So am I. I <u>enjoy</u> a good Western as well.
Jane:	Oh, do you? I <u>don't</u>. I <u>can't</u> <u>stand</u> them because of the violence. I <u>like</u> romantic films.
Tom:	So do I, especially the good old-fashioned ones.

b Work in pairs and practise this dialogue. Take it in turns to be Jane and Tom.

2 Model Phrases

Follow the procedure outlined in the Introduction (page 5) about model phrases. Get the class to start practising the model phrases using the 'likes' and 'dislikes' discussed earlier in the Presentation exercise.

3 Notes

Explain the following points carefully:

a The use of the gerund form after 'enjoy', 'like', 'love', 'fond of', 'keen on', etc. when using a verb.

b All the phrases can be followed by either the gerund form or a noun,

e.g. I like tennis.
playing squash.

(Although 'enjoy' is more frequently used with the gerund.)

c The use of So do I   to agree with what has been expressed.
So can they
Neither does he
Nor has he

(Where a class is unfamiliar with this usage in English pre-teach it in a grammar lesson to avoid too many lengthy explanations in this unit.)

d The technique for contradicting the speaker to express the opposite to his/her taste by using the phrases:

Do you? I don't.
Don't you? I do.

2 Model Phrases

Likes			Agree	Disagree
I	like love enjoy	going to the cinema. Chinese food.	So do I.	Do you? I don't.
I'm	keen on comedy films. fond of playing football.		So am I.	Are you? I'm not.

Dislikes		Agree	Disagree
I don't like	housework. getting up early.	Neither do I.	Don't you? I do.
I can't stand	disco music. waiting for the bus.	Neither can I.	Can't you? I can.
I'm not keen on	swimming. classical music.	Neither am I.	Aren't you? I am.
I hate	cold weather. travelling by bus.	So do I.	Do you? I don't.

3 Notes

a Note the '-ing' form after these verbs: 'like', 'love', 'enjoy', 'keen on', 'fond of', 'can't stand', 'hate', e.g.:

I love dancing but I can't stand playing tennis.

b Note the order of the words to agree/disagree:

So do I.
Neither have they.
Nor can he.

4 Pronunciation

Points to notice are:

a The emphasis is on the activity or thing which is liked, e.g.:

    I like playing tennis.

b The rise and fall of:

    Do you? I don't.

    Are you? I'm not.

c The pronunciation of 'of' [əv] and the stress on the activity in the phrase:

    I'm fond of walking.

d The pronunciation of 'for' = [fə] in the phrase:

    I hate shopping for food.

e A slight emphasis on 'stand' in the phrase:

    I can't stand writing letters.

f The pronunciation of 'can' [kən] in the phrases:

    Neither can I.
    Nor can he.

5 Fluency Practice Exercises

a Divide the students into pairs and explain the two columns – in the right-hand column there are various likes and dislikes and in the left-hand one there are responses. Explain that there may be several possible responses to any one statement but remind them to be careful to make sure that the answer chosen is suitable and correct. If necessary practise one or two all together first to establish the pattern. Ensure that they take turns at using the columns.

b Tell the students to look at the table with the illustrations and explain that they have to put a tick (✓) if they like what is depicted or a cross (X) if they don't under the four headings for Films, Sports, Travelling and Collecting. When they have completed the table divide them into pairs and using the dialogue given under the table as an example tell them to make up short dialogues in a similar way, according to what they have put down. This exercise is free oral practice and could be recorded on video camera or tape where facilities are available or written down by each pair and performed orally for the rest of the class.

c Not, the negative form used to agree with a negative statement:

	Response
I don't like swimming.	Neither do I
I'm not fond of olives.	Nor am I

d Don't repeat the main verb again in the reply, use 'do', 'does', e.g.:

	Response
I like football.	So do I. (*Not* So do I like.)

e But repeat 'can', 'am', 'has', 'will', 'must' in the reply, e.g.:

	Response
I can't stand tennis.	Neither can I.
I'm fond of chocolate.	So is she.

4 Pronunciation

Now listen carefully and repeat.

5 Fluency Practice Exercises

a With a partner use the table below to suggest likes and dislikes. One will choose a phrase from the left column and the other will give a suitable answer from the right column. Take turns at this.

I like romantic films.	Isn't he? I am.
Jane loves tennis.	So is Fred.
I'm keen on golf.	Neither are they.
He can't stand fish and chips.	So does Mary.
I enjoy black coffee.	So are we.
She hates going to the opera.	Nor can I.
John doesn't like beer.	Does she? I don't.
He's not keen on horror films.	Neither does Jane.
Mary is fond of yellow.	Do you? Fred doesn't.
Jack likes watching TV.	Aren't they? I am.
They're not fond of picnics.	So do they.
She can't stand pop music.	Do you? So does John.
They don't like pizza.	Are you? So are we.
They're not keen on football.	So does my brother.
I don't like beer.	So do I.
I can't stand old movies.	Is she? So am I.
He's keen on golf.	Can't you?
Susan doesn't like disco music.	Neither can we.

b Look at the table and under each picture put a tick (✓) if you like it or a cross (X) if you don't like it.

6 Further Practice

This group activity provides extensive practice for the students to ask as well as answer questions about likes and dislikes and also to express them in the third person at the report-back stage. In the Student's Book there is part of a Questionnaire with sample answers but the students in the groups have to make up the rest of it. Tell each group to write their questions on a separate sheet of paper using the headings given and to add two more of their own choice. Spaces for only three suggested names are shown in the book but they should add several more names. When they have completed their Questionnaires tell each member of the group to interview a number of students in other groups (or even other classes where possible) and fill in the answers. Pre-teach the question 'What kind of sports/music/books do you like/enjoy/dislike?' if necessary. When they have completed their Questionnaires they should report back on their findings either using individual names, group reference names, or whatever the teacher thinks is appropriate, e.g.:

Maria can't stand going to the launderette.
Half the people in group 4 like skiing.
Three out of eight people I interviewed are fond of classical music.
Nick doesn't like Chinese food but Fred does.

F I L M S

WESTERNS ☐ HORROR ☐   CRIME ☐ ROMANTIC ☐

S P O R T S

TENNIS ☐   SKIING ☐   SWIMMING ☐ FOOTBALL ☐

T R A V E L L I N G

CAR ☐   BUS ☐   SHIP ☐   PLANE ☐

C O L L E C T I N G

STAMPS ☐   COINS ☐   BOTTLES ☐ RECORDS ☐

Then with a partner talk about the different things and give suitable responses, e.g.:

A: I like romantic films.
B: I'm fond of them, too. I love thrillers as well.
A: So do I. I'm keen on Westerns, too.
B: So is my brother.
A: I can't stand travelling by bus.
B: Neither can I. And I hate going by plane.
A: So do I. I'm not keen on trains.
B: Nor am I.

6 Further Practice

In small groups make a questionnaire like this about Sports, TV, Music and two other subjects and use it to ask the others in the class questions. Fill it with model phrases as in the examples:

Name of student	Sports	TV	Pop Music		
Maria	Keen on cycling can't stand tennis				
Hans		can't stand *Dallas* fond of the news			
Yoshi					

Then give a report about their likes and dislikes, e.g.:

Maria can't stand tennis but Hans is fond of the news on TV., etc.

/121/

Unit 11   Telephoning

Students may find that they will need English when using the telephone both in their personal and professional lives. The aim of this unit is to provide them with the language to answer the telephone, leave and take messages, and perform a variety of other functions necessary for this purpose.

See Introduction for instructions on how to use each exercise.

Unit 11

Telephoning

1 Presentation

a Follow the procedure outlined in the Introduction (page 4) about relevant expressions. Before playing the cassette discuss with the students the situations in which they would need to use the telephone. Explain that they will hear five short telephone conversations and pre-teach any unfamiliar vocabulary.

b Divide the students into pairs and tell them to practise the dialogues each taking a part in turns.

1 Presentation

a Listen to these short telephone conversations and fill in the spaces:

i | A: Bournemouth 51756.
B: Could I speak to Frances, please?

ii | A: Hello.
B: Hello, could I speak to Mr Black, please?
A: This is Mr Black speaking.
B: This is Mrs Walker.

iii | A: Hello.
B: Hello, can I speak to Liz, please?
A: I'm sorry, she's out now. Is there any message?
B: Could you tell her John rang?
A: All right.

iv | A: Good morning, Royal Park Hotel. Can I help you?
B: Good morning. Could I speak to Mr Charles King, please? He's in Room 526.
A: Who's calling, please?
B: This is Mrs King.
A: Hold on, please.

v | A: Hello, Pascoe's Office Supplies.
B: Hello, could I speak to Mrs Grant, please?
A: I'm afraid she's not available at the moment. Who's calling?
B: This is Mr Freeman of Newton and Company. Could you ask her to call me back?
A: Yes, certainly, Mr Freeman. Goodbye.

b In pairs practise reading the dialogues. Take turns at this.

2 Model Phrases

Follow the procedure outlined in the Introduction (page 5) about model phrases. As a revision of familiar material point out how phrases previously learnt such as 'I'm afraid', 'could I', 'could you', and 'would you like to', are used in the context. Explain that 'hang on' and 'hold on' are used in general language to mean 'wait for a short time' and are not only used in telephoning.

3 Notes

a Stress to the class the use of 'double' when two figures are the same in a telephone number and if necessary practise with a few examples by writing them on the board and asking the class, e.g.:
78544   What's this number?
It's 7–8–5–double–4.

b Point out that it's possible to say 'Speaking' when you have been asked for by name:
Is that Mr Andrews?
Speaking.

4 Pronunciation

Points to notice are:

a Slight emphasis on the name and the rising tone for the question, e.g.:

Could I speak to Mr Smith?

b Slight emphasis on 'speaking' in the response, e.g.:

This is Mr Smith speaking.

c A rising intonation in the question

Who's calling, please?

d Emphasis on 'on' and 'get', e.g.:
Hold on a minute ... I'll get her.

e A rising intonation in

Can [kən] you give him a message, please?

f Stress on the name, e.g.:
Mrs Turner isn't available [əveɪləbəl].

2 Model Phrases

a Asking for someone:
 Could I ⎱ speak to Mr Langdon, please?
 Can I ⎰ talk to Bob, please?

b Identifying yourself:
 This is Mark (speaking).
 Susan speaking.

c Waiting:
 Hang on
 Hold on while I get him/her.

 Just a moment.
 Just a minute.

d Not available:

 I'm sorry, he's/she's out.
 I'm sorry, he's/she's not available.

 He's/she's busy at the moment.

e Messages:
 Is there any message?
 Would you like to leave a message?
 Could you ask him/her to call me?
 Could you tell him/her . . .?

3 Notes

a In a telephone number when you have two numbers the same together e.g. 55048, you say, 'double five-oh-four-eight'.
b When you answer the phone and somebody asks for you by name you reply:
  i This is Maria/Fred (speaking).
  ii Speaking.

 You do not say:
  Here is Maria/Fred.

4 Pronunciation

Now listen carefully and repeat.

5 Fluency Practice Exercises

a Divide the students into pairs and tell them to write out the sentences in the three sets of boxes into telephone conversations. When they have written the lines in the correct order tell the students to practise reading them aloud, perhaps sitting back to back to increase the realism of the telephoning situation where the caller can't be seen. If available record these on a video camera or a cassette and go over them all together afterwards. Check carefully that the lines are in a logical order.

b Unlike the other Fluency Practice Exercises this one is partly on cassette. Before playing the cassette tell the students to imagine they are on the telephone and that they will hear two complete dialogues and then one half of a dialogue for the next two. They have to make suitable responses or ask appropriate questions. There are prompts in the Student's Book giving them the necessary information but they have to construct the correct sentences or questions. The first two dialogues (i, ii) are partly given in the Student's Book and they must fill in the blank spaces. Allow time for the class to think before playing the cassette. Explain that in dialogues iii and iv the students will hear one half of the conversation, B, written out in the right-hand column, and that in the left-hand column they will find prompts, A, for the other half of the conversation. Allow plenty of time for the class to study the information and work out what to say. Discuss possible alternatives that they may come up with as further reinforcement of the material.

5 Fluency Practice Exercises

a With a partner use these phrases to make short telephone dialogues. They are not in order. Take turns at this.

i	5 Would you like to play tennis tomorrow afternoon? 3 It's Tim here. 1 Can I speak to Mike, please? 7 Good, I'll see you at the courts at 5.30.	2 This is Mike speaking. 6 Yes, I'd love to. 8 That's fine. Goodbye. 4 Hello, Tim.
ii	5 Hold the line please, I'll put you through. 3 Who's calling? 1 Good morning, Denne and Company. 7 Go ahead, please. You're through.	4 This is Mrs Clark. 6 Thank you. 2 Could I speak to Mr Jackson?
iii	3 I'm afraid she's out. 1 55013. 5 Yes, of course.	4 Can you give her a message, please? 6 Could you tell her Phil rang and ask her to call me later? 2 Could I speak to Jenny, please?

b Listen to the two telephone dialogues, i and ii. Then, in pairs, go through both dialogues using the Instruction prompts to help you fill in the gaps.

Instructions

i A: Your number is 58096.

A: Janet is out. Offer to give her a message.

A: Agree and say goodbye.

Dialogue

(*Ring ..... ring ..... ring .....*)
A: Hello, 58096.
B: Could I speak to Janet, please?
A: I'm sorry but she's out. Would you like to leave a message?
B: Could you ask her to phone Mrs Brandon this evening, please?
A: Yes, of course. Goodbye.

ii *You telephone Parker and Company*

  A: You want Mr Mansfield.

  A: Your name is Les Winter.

  A: Ask for Mr Mansfield to phone. Your number is 833263.

  A: Respond.

(*Ring ..... ring ..... ring .....*)
B: Parker and Company. Can I help you?
A: <u>Could</u> I <u>speak</u> to Mr Mansfield, please?
B: Who's calling, please?
A: <u>This</u> <u>is</u> Les Winter <u>speaking</u>.
B: Hang on. I'm sorry, Mr Mansfield isn't in his office at the moment. Is there any message?
A: <u>Could</u> you ask him to <u>call</u> <u>me</u> as soon as possible? My <u>number</u> is 833263.
B: Yes, of course. Goodbye.
A: <u>Goodbye.</u>

Now you will hear half of the telephone dialogues, iii and iv, and you must respond using the instruction prompts on the left. Give the complete response for A.

iii *You phone the Regal Cinema*

  A: Ask which film is on.

  A: Ask what time it starts.

  A: Ask when the last show finishes.

  A: Respond.

(*Ring ..... ring ..... ring ...*)
B: Good morning. Regal Cinema.
A:
B: This week it's *Rocky 3*.
A:
B: At 2.15, 4.25, 6.45 and 9.00.
A:
B: At about 11.15.
A:

iv *You phone a restaurant*

  A: Book a table for Saturday evening.

  A: You want to eat at 7.30.

  A: Choose which time you want.

  A: It's for five people.

  A: Give your name.

(*Ring ..... ring ..... ring*)
B: Good evening .... Tavernetta restaurant.
A:
B: Certainly, what time?
A:
B: I'm sorry but we're completely booked then. But I can give you a table at 6.45 or at 8.15.
A:
B: Certainly, and how many people?
A:
B: Mmm ... and the name, please?
A:
B: Thank you. We look forward to seeing you on Saturday.

6 Situations

Please refer to the Introduction (page 7).

Suggested Answers

a Could I speak to the manager, please?
b I'm sorry he's/she's not here at the moment. Could I take a message?
c Speaking.
d Just a minute while I get my diary.
e Could you ask him/her to call me this evening after 8 o'clock – my number is 76509.
f Could you tell me the times of the trains to London/Birmingham on Saturday morning, please?
g Could you tell me the exchange rate for dollars, please?

6 Situations

a You telephone a shop and want the manager. What would you say?

b Someone rings up to speak to your friend but he/she is not at home. What would you say?

c You answer the telephone and someone asks for you by name. What do you say?

d You are speaking to a friend on the phone and need to get your diary to check a date. What would you say?

e You ring up a friend but he/she's not there. You want to leave a message for him/her to ring you later. What would you say?

f You telephone the train station to find out the time of the trains to the nearest big city. What do you say?

g You phone the bank to find out the exchange rate for dollars. What do you say?

Unit 12   Instructions

The aim of this unit is to teach students the necessary language to give and understand precise instructions about how to use or operate simple machinery, electrical equipment and telephones and how to prepare meals and do a variety of other everyday things.

See Introduction for instructions on how to use each exercise.

Unit 12

Instructions

1 Presentation

a Follow the procedure outlined in the Introduction (page 4) about relevant expressions. Briefly discuss with the class if they know how to make a pot of tea and pre-teach any necessary vocabulary such as 'boil', 'teapot', etc. Tell the students they will hear a dialogue in which one person is explaining to another how to make a pot of tea and that they have to fill in the spaces provided.

b Divide the class into pairs and tell them each to take the part of Tom or Jane and to practise reading the dialogue to each other, taking it in turns. If the necessary facilities are available provide a pair of students with a teapot, kettle, etc. and tell them to practise the dialogue in the real situation in front of the class.

1 Presentation

a Listen to Jane and Tom's conversation. She is telling him how to make a pot of tea. Follow the instructions and fill in the spaces.

Tom	Jane
I'd like to know how to make a pot of tea. What do you do first?	Well, first of all you have to fill the kettle with fresh water and boil it, of course.
Oh, yes . . . and then?	Then you put a little hot water in the teapot to warm it.
And next?	Next you put in the tea.
Mmmmm . . . how much?	A teaspoonful for each person and one for the pot.
What's next?	When the water is boiling you pour it into the teapot.
Right. And then?	Then you let the tea stand for a couple of minutes.
What do you do next?	Last of all you drink it with sugar and milk or lemon.

b In pairs practise this dialogue and take turns at being Tom or Jane.

2 Model Phrases

Follow the procedure outlined in the Introduction (page 5) about model phrases. Draw pictures to run through the phrases used to illustrate the sequence of steps in making the pot of tea.

3 Notes

a Explain that there are different forms of the verb which can be used to give the instructions, e.g.:
  i Imperative: 'Boil'.
  ii Simple present: 'You boil'.
  iii With 'have to': 'You have to boil'.

4 Pronunciation

Points to notice are:

a 'of' [əv] in the phrases 'first of all', 'last of all' and a slight emphasis on the words 'first' and 'last'.

b Emphasis on the word 'first' in the phrase 'the first thing you add ...'

c The elision of 'next step' [nəkstep] with the 't' of 'next' virtually disappearing.

d 'and' [ənd] in the phrases 'and then', 'and finally', with emphasis placed on the words 'then' and 'finally'.

5 Fluency Practice Exercises

a i Divide the students into pairs and tell them that one has to ask how to use a payphone and the other has to explain. Tell them to use the model phrases and the words in the table to ask and answer in the form of a dialogue where each of the stages is explained one by one. Pre-teach any vocabulary that may be unfamiliar such as 'dial', 'receiver', 'insert', etc., so that the students know what they have to do. The dialogue should begin something like this:

A: What do I do first of all?
B: First you (have to) pick up the receiver.
A: And then what do I do after that?
B: Next/then you ...

  ii Follow the same procedure exactly for this part but ensure that the students change roles so that each one practises making questions and giving instructions.

2 Model Phrases

Question	Instruction

What do you do first (of all?)
 	
And then?
    next?
And third?
    fourth?
What's next?
	First (of all) you put ...
	                have to put ...
	Then put ...
	Next you have to put ...
	After that put ...
	            you have to put ...
	Last of all put ...
	Finally you have to put ...

3 Notes

a When giving instructions you can do it three different ways:

First   you boil   the kettle.
           boil
           you have to boil

b As an introduction to giving instructions you can say:

This is how you do it.

4 Pronunciation

Now listen carefully and repeat.

5 Fluency Practice Exercises

a With a partner look at the instructions. One person will ask the questions from the left column and the other will answer from the right column.

i Using a Pay Telephone:

Questions	Instructions
First of all	Pick up the receiver
After that	Listen for the dialling tone
Then	Insert the correct money
Next	Dial the number
After that	The telephone rings
Then	Speak

b Divide the students into pairs and explain that they have to ask for and give instructions about how to use a coffee machine. Pre-teach any unfamiliar vocabulary and discuss briefly if they know how to use such a machine. Allow plenty of time for the students to look at the pictures and tell them to construct questions to ask for the instructions and to answer using the model phrases appropriately. Point out that some of the prompts are given.

6 Further Practice

Find out from the students if they know how to make local and regional dishes or drinks. In pairs or small groups tell them to work out a set of suitable instructions to make one of these, with suitable diagrams if possible. These could be written down or recorded on cassette, or video if available, and then given to the other groups for comparison and criticism.

7 Situations

Please refer to the Introduction (page 7). The situations in this unit are slightly more complex than in the previous units. Pre-teach any vocabulary that the students may require, limit them to three or four sentences per situation and remind them to use the model phrases. This could be done as a written exercise for homework.

Suggested Answers

a First of all you switch on the recorder. Then you press the button to open the lid; next you put in the cassette in the right way; then you close the lid; finally you press the start button.

b First you put some water in a saucepan; then you put the pan on the cooker and turn it on; next you heat the water until it boils; then you put the egg in the saucepan and let the water boil for three to six minutes (for soft or hard boiled eggs); finally you remove the egg from the pan.

c First you grind the coffee; then you put the right amount of water in the coffee machine; next you put the coffee in the filter; then you switch on the machine and wait for the coffee to percolate; finally you switch it off and pour the coffee into a cup.

d First of all you get a hammer and some nails; then you choose the place for the picture and mark the spot on the wall; next you hammer a nail into the wall; finally you hang the picture on the nail.

ii Changing Batteries in a Cassette Recorder:

Questions	Instructions
First	Take off the battery cover
Then	Take out the batteries
Next	Put in the new batteries
After that	Put back the battery cover
Then	Check that the recorder works

b Working in pairs look at the pictures about how to use a coffee machine. One student will ask the questions and the other will give the instructions. Take turns at this. We have done the first one for you.

A: What do you do first?

B: First of all you put in the money.

A: _____

B: _____

A: And then?

B: _____

A: _____

B: _____

A: _____

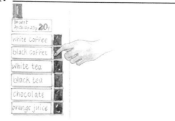

B: _____

6 Further Practice

In pairs or small groups explain how to make special food/dishes/drinks from your country or region.

7 Situations

a Explain how to operate a cassette recorder.
b Give instructions for boiling an egg.
c Give instructions for making a good cup of coffee.
d Explain how to hang a picture or a poster on the wall.

Revision Units 7 – 12

1 At a Party

The first section of this second revision unit covers Unit 8 (Invitations), Unit 11 (Telephoning), Unit 7 (Making Offers) as well as any incidental phrases which may be useful in the situations. If necessary briefly revise the relevant units before beginning the exercises to refresh the students' memories.

a Briefly discuss with the students the arrangements that would be necessary before giving a party and write them on the board. Also include the various kinds of parties, e.g. formal, informal, birthday, anniversary, new house, celebration, etc. Divide the class into small groups of three or four and tell each group that they are planning a party. Tell them to decide what kind of party they want to give and to plan the date, time, place and people they want to invite. Tell each person to make a role card with information about name, age, family, job, address, and so on. (See Revision Units 1–6, page 78 for a model.) Check that the groups all know what to do and then when they have prepared everything each group should 'telephone' people from the other groups who will act as 'guests'. Remind them to use the phrases from Units 8 for invitations and 11 for telephoning.

b In the same groups as before tell each student to take it in turns to act as a host or hostess and offer food and drink to the other guests. Use the information from the role cards for names and any other suitable information during this stage. To add realism supply plates, glasses and other objects and if possible video or record each 'performance' for critical appraisal afterwards.

c This should be done immediately after part 1b to make a whole role play out of the situation. After offering to wash up and do other things in the host's/hostess's home (using the paper plates, glasses, etc. if available) tell the students to offer to take other 'guests' home and check the addresses from the role cards.

2 TV Survey

Revision practice for Unit 9 (Asking for Permission) and Unit 10 (Likes and Dislikes) is provided in this question on the theme of a television survey. Discuss with the students the kind of television programmes they like to watch and write them on the board to help them with creating their own survey questionnaires. Divide them into small groups and tell them to look at the sample questionnaire given in the Student's Book, and then tell them to draw up their own using it as a model. When they have done this tell each student to interview other students and to put a tick ($\checkmark$) in the box which describes their feelings. Remind the students to use the phrases in Unit 9 for asking for permission before they question another student. When they have finished tell each group

Revision Units 7 – 12

Unit 7   Making Offers

Unit 8   Invitations

Unit 9   Asking for Permission

Unit 10   Likes and Dislikes

Unit 11   Telephoning

Unit 12   Instructions

1 a In small groups plan a party. Decide on the type of party, the date and time, the place and how many people. Then in pairs telephone the guests to invite them to the party. Use the phrases for invitations from Unit 8 and for telephoning from Unit 11.

b In small groups each person will take turns being the host or hostess and offer the guests something to eat and drink and they will accept or refuse. Use the phrases from Unit 7 for offering and accepting/ refusing.

c At the end of the party the guests will offer to help the host or hostess and also offer to take the other guests home. Use the phrases from Unit 7 to help you.

2 In small groups prepare a list of questions to ask about the viewers' responses to different types of television programmes and make a questionnaire. Here is a sample to help make out your own questionnaire and you can think of other types of programmes:

Programme	Keen on	Like	Don't like	Can't stand
News				
Sports				
Comedies				
Films				
Documentaries				

to prepare a report on the responses they have got from the other groups using the phrases from Unit 10 for likes and dislikes in this way, e.g.:

Out of twelve people interviewed:

Six people are very fond of the news.
Two people can't stand sports programmes.
One person likes comedies very much.

3 Staying with a Family

a The phrases in Unit 9 (Asking for Permission) are covered by this section. Explain that in this situation the students have to imagine they are staying with a family or a friend in England. Discuss briefly the kinds of things that they would need to ask permission for when staying in an unfamiliar house and write them on the board. Then divide them into pairs and tell them to study the pictures. (When a picture is crossed out it means that permission is not given.) Tell each pair to take the different parts in turn. They could supply extra pictures of their own for the other groups for further practice if required.

b This exercise revises the phrases in Unit 12 (Instructions). Tell the students to work out how to operate the video and if necessary make notes. Discuss the various stages all together and supply any vocabulary they may need before they begin. Tell them to do this in dialogue form with the guest interjecting phrases such as

What do you do first?
What comes next?
And then?

This could be recorded on cassette or on video and then discussed afterwards.

c Divide the class into pairs and tell them to study the situations. This section practises the phrases from Unit 11 (Telephoning). Then tell them to telephone each other taking it in turns to be the caller. For further practice encourage them to think of more situations of their own for the others to use.

Ask five other students in the class and mark their responses with a tick
(√) if they like or a cross (X) if they dislike the programmes, e.g.:
  What do you think of . . .?
  What's your opinion of . . .?

They must answer using the model phrases. Then check the results and
present a report about the responses for each programme, e.g.:
  Three out of five people like sports.
  Two of the people can't stand the films.

Use the phrases on the questionnaire to reply. Use the phrases in Unit 9
for asking for permission to interview the others and the phrases in Unit
10 for likes and dislikes.

3 a You have just arrived in England to stay with a family for several
weeks. Your hostess/friend shows you around the house and you ask
if you can do the things in the pictures. Work in pairs with one as the
student and the other as the hostess/friend who will respond. (X
across the picture = refuse.)

Use the phrases in Unit 9 for asking for permission.

b You do not know how to use the video recorder so ask your
hostess/friend to give you instructions. Work in pairs and one will ask
and the other will explain. Use the phrases for instructions from Unit
12.

c Work in pairs and do these telephone dialogues. One student will
phone and the other will reply. Take turns at this.

  i Phone the school and ask to speak to your teacher. Explain that
  you are ill and can't come to class.
  ii Call a classmate's home and ask to speak to him/her. Then ask
  what happened in the lesson when you were absent.
  iii Phone your hostess/friend and explain that you will arrive home
  late.
  iv Call a friend and invite him/her for dinner next weekend.
  v Call a friend to arrange to meet at 8p.m. tomorrow; he/she is not
  home so leave a message.

Use the phrases for telephoning from Unit 11.

4 Filling your Diary

This section revises the phrases for Unit 8 (Invitations). Tell the class to look at the cutaway page of a diary in the Student's Book and to make a whole page with six activities for the whole week, Monday to Sunday. There are three examples given but discuss with the students all together the kinds of activities they might put in before they write anything down. Tell them to scatter the activities they choose over the various days and to write down the exact time they will be doing each activity. When they have completed the diary divide them into small groups. Tell them to invite the others in the group to the activities they have chosen and they will accept or refuse according to whether they have something else written down in their own diary or not. Ensure that the students take turns at asking and responding.

5 Instructions

Further revision practice for the phrases in Unit 12 (Instructions) is provided in this exercise. Divide the class into groups and assign each group an individual task from the list of three or let them choose for themselves. Tell them to prepare appropriate instructions for their task and give them any additional help they may require with vocabulary. Get them to draw pictures to accompany their instructions where possible and when they have completed their task ask each group to present their completed set of instructions to the rest of the class for comment. This could be recorded on cassette or video and then discussed afterwards.

4 Make a diary like the one below with six activities and times for the whole week, Monday to Sunday. Then divide into small groups and take it in turns to invite the others who will accept or refuse. Use the phrases for inviting, accepting and refusing from Unit 8.

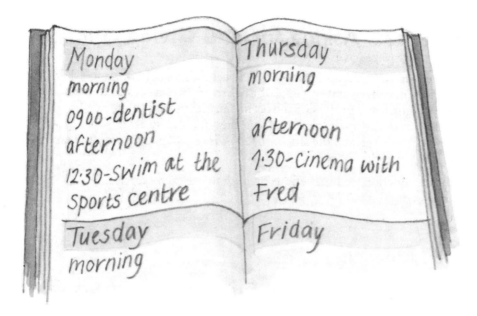

Monday
morning
0900-dentist
afternoon
12:30-Swim at the
Sports centre
Tuesday
morning

Thursday
morning

afternoon
1:30-Cinema with
Fred

Friday

5 In groups explain how to do the following:

a Make an omelette.
b Record a programme on a radio cassette recorder.
c Change the refill in a ballpoint pen.

Use the phrases for instructions in Unit 12.

Unit 13 Asking for and Giving Opinions

In everyday conversation people often need to give opinions and ask for the opinions of others, and students of English are no exception. In the case of their personal and professional lives in discussion with their friends, colleagues or classmates they will find they want to know how to say what they think or feel, and the aim of this unit is to equip them with the essential language to fulfil this need.

See Introduction for instructions on how to use each exercise.

1 Presentation

a Follow the procedure outlined in the Introduction (page 4) about relevant expressions. To introduce the unit elicit from the students their opinions on a variety of topics of everyday interest, e.g. the weather, local politics or events, a recent film or TV programme, a new fashion in clothes or hair styles and so on and briefly discuss them. Explain that there are two columns in the table and eight short dialogues on the cassette – the first column is for the question that is used to ask for an opinion and the second for the opinion given in response.

b Divide the students into pairs and tell them to practise the dialogues themselves using the table, taking it in turns to ask and answer.

Unit 13

Asking for and Giving Opinions

Presentation

a Listen to the tape and fill in the spaces:

	Question	Opinion
i	What <u>do you think</u> of people smoking in restaurants?	I think it's <u>terrible</u>.
ii	<u>What's your</u> opinion <u>of</u> children wearing school uniforms?	Well, I don't think <u>they should really</u>.
iii	<u>Do you think</u> children should get pocket money?	Well, I'm <u>afraid</u> <u>I don't</u> really.
iv	<u>What do you think</u> of national military service?	I think it's a <u>very good idea</u>.
v	<u>Do you think</u> watching TV is bad for children?	Well, it's <u>not too bad</u>.
vi	<u>What's your</u> opinion of driving at age 16?	I really <u>don't think they</u> should.
vii	Do <u>you like</u> the idea of voting at age 18?	Yes, I do. I think <u>it's a good idea</u>.
viii	<u>What do you think</u> about the drug problem nowadays?	<u>In my</u> opinion it's terrible.

b Work in pairs and practise these dialogues. Take it in turns to ask and answer.

2 Model Phrases

Follow the procedure outlined in the Introduction (page 5) about model phrases.

a Asking for Opinions

Point out that the first and second phrases ask for opinions about actions or activities, e.g. smoking, driving too fast, playing sports; the third and fourth phrases ask for opinions about things, e.g. 'new dress', 'TV programme', 'a book'.

b Giving Opinions

Ask the students where they think these opinions would be used and which would be suitable responses to the phrases in Part 2a and which would not. Point out the use of 'I'm afraid' to mean 'I'm sorry'.

3 Notes

a The response to 'Do you like ...?' is 'Yes, I do' or 'No, I'm afraid I don't' or 'No, I don't'.

It's unusual for people to repeat the word 'opinion' in a phrase in response to the question 'What's your opinion of ...?'; they usually choose an alternative phrase for the reply.

b British people tend not to disagree very abruptly with each other's opinions as it can cause offence. Although not necessarily a uniquely British attribute, it may seem strange and needs to be explained to students who want to visit Britain. For this reason the three phrases in the list are important and may need a little supplementary explanation from the teacher.

c The verb 'think' with the prepositions 'of/about' is followed by an object person plus the gerund, and the question 'What's your opinion of ...?' uses the same structure with object person and gerund.

2 Model Phrases

a Asking for Opinions

Do you think people should smoke in public places?
What's your opinion of children watching television?
Do you like my new car?
What do you think of the new Star Wars film?

b Giving Opinions

Yes I do. I think it's marvellous/great/a good idea.
Well, it's not too bad.
Well, I'm afraid I don't really.
I don't like it at all!
I think it's really fantastic/interesting.
In my opinion it's terrible/wonderful.
Well, I don't think they should really.
I think it's a good/bad idea.
I'm afraid I don't think it's a good idea.

3 Notes

a Notice the answers:

	Response
Do you like black coffee?	Yes, I do.
	(*Not* Yes, I like.)
	No, I don't.
	(*Not* No, I don't like.)
What's your opinion of . . .?	I think . . .
	(*Not* My opinion is . . .)

b In Britain it can be impolite to disagree too strongly with another opinion. If you don't agree you should say:

Well, it's not too bad.
I'm afraid I don't.
I'm not sure about it.

c Notice this construction:

think of/about
opinion of $+$ someone $+$ doing something, e.g.:

What do you think $\begin{smallmatrix} \text{of} \\ \text{about} \end{smallmatrix}$ people smoking in restaurants?

What's your opinion of children watching violence on TV?

4 Pronunciation

Points to notice:

a The contracted form 'D'you' and the word 'should' [ʃəd] with the rising tone of the question.

b The stress in the word 'fantastic'.

c The pronunciation of 'of' [əv] in the phrase:
   What do you think of the film?

d The stress in the word 'opinion' and the word 'of' [əv] and the rising tone of the question in the phrase:

What's your opinion of children watching TV?

5 Fluency Practice Exercises

a Divide the students into pairs and explain that they have to choose a suitable response from the right-hand column to an opinion expressed from the left-hand column. Explain that although not all answers are possible there may be several alternative responses. Go over the various possibilities at the end when they have finished.

4 Pronunciation

Now listen carefully and repeat.

5 Fluency Practice Exercises

a In pairs use the table to practise asking for and giving opinions. One will ask and the other will give an opinion. There are several possibilities.

Do you like my pullover?	Yes, I do.
What do you think of pop music?	I think it's lovely.
What's your opinion of cats?	In my opinion it's terrible.
Do you think young girls should wear make-up?	Yes, I think it's fantastic.
What do you think of science fiction films?	Well, I'm afraid I don't.
What's your opinion of rock and roll music?	I don't think they should.
Do you like poetry?	Well, I think it's a bit old-fashioned.
Do you think people should vote at 18?	Well, I'm afraid it's not a good idea.
What do you think about people eating meat?	I think they're wonderful.
What's your opinion of this best seller?	I don't really like them.

b Divide the students into pairs and explain that in turns they have to ask for each other's opinions about the things in the three parts and then answer. Tell them to use full answers instead of 'Yes' or 'No' and when they have finished discuss with the class all together some of the opinions given to make a comparison.

6 Further Practice

Divide the students into pairs or small groups and explain that they have to prepare a plan for an Activity Centre for children, young people, adults and retired people in the town. Elicit from them the kind of facilities such a centre would offer and briefly discuss the possibilities. Tell them in their groups or pairs to think of more ideas of their own and to draw up a list; also, each group should prepare a floor plan of the centre to show where the various activities would take place. Go around and advise each group on their ideas if necessary. When they have worked out their ideas and plan tell them to make a presentation to the rest of the students who should give their opinions about the proposals. The presenters should also invite opinions from the rest of the class to practise using both aspects of the Unit. Ask the students to choose the best plan at the end of the exercise and give reasons for their choice.

b Work in pairs and take turns to ask and reply to the questions below:

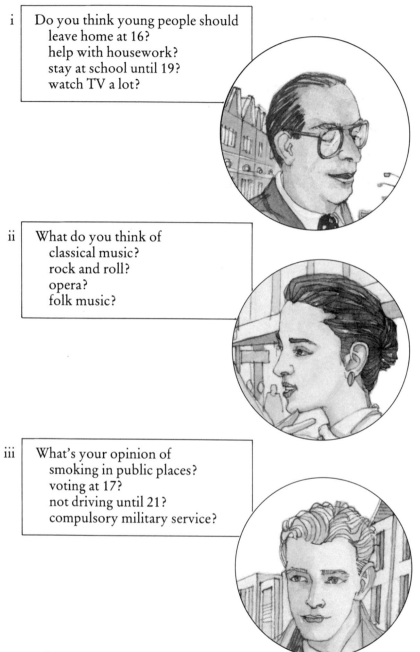

i | Do you think young people should
leave home at 16?
help with housework?
stay at school until 19?
watch TV a lot?

ii | What do you think of
classical music?
rock and roll?
opera?
folk music?

iii | What's your opinion of
smoking in public places?
voting at 17?
not driving until 21?
compulsory military service?

6 Further Practice

In pairs or small groups make a plan of an Activity Centre for your town. Your centre is for children, young people, adults and retired· people so you must think of different activities to interest them. Make a list of suggestions (e.g. sports, entertainment, clubs) and give your ideas to the others in your group. They will give their opinions. Finally draw a plan and present it to the rest of the class.

7 Situations

Please refer to the Introduction (page 7).

Suggested Answers

a I'm afraid I don't really like it.
b I don't think it's a very practical idea.
c I think it's a complete waste of time and money.
d I think your new hair style is terrific!
e I don't like it at all!
f I thought it was very interesting.
g I think it's really delicious!
h I'm afraid it's a terrible situation at the moment.

7 Situations

a A friend asks your opinion of her new dress. You don't really like it. What do you say?

b At a party someone tells you that he thinks food should be free for everyone. What do you say?

c Somebody asks what you think of advertising on television. Give your opinion.

d Your friend has just had a new hair style and asks what you think of it. You think it's terrific. What do you say?

e A man in the street asks you to try a new product for market research. You try it but think it's horrible. What do you say?

f A colleague at work asks what you thought about the sales conference you went to last week. Give your opinion.

g You are having dinner at a friend's house and you really like the food. What do you say when the host asks for your opinion?

h At a party someone asks what you think of the world economic situation. What do you say?

Unit 14   Agreeing and Disagreeing

Users of any language will often get into situations where they discuss things and the relevant language to agree or to disagree without causing offence is absolutely indispensable in such cases. This unit aims to provide the necessary language for this skill and a variety of situations for extensive practice.

See Introduction for instructions on how to use each exercise.

Unit 14

Agreeing and Disagreeing

1 Presentation

a Follow the procedure outlined in the Introduction (page 4) about relevant expressions. Before playing the cassette discuss with the students their various opinions about sport and elicit from them whether they agree or disagree, e.g. that sport is valuable, that there is too much/not enough on TV, and so on. Tell them that they will hear one conversation in which two people, Tom and Jane, are discussing sport and agreeing and disagreeing with what is said.

b Divide the students into pairs and tell them to read the dialogue taking it in turns to be Jane or Tom.

1 Presentation

a Listen to the dialogue between Tom and Jane and fill in the spaces:

Tom	Well, Jane, I think sport is good for you and everybody should take exercise.
Jane	I quite agree, Tom.
Tom	Too many people sit in their offices all day. They don't get out and do anything to keep fit!
Jane	You're absolutely right.
Tom	The main reason for heart attacks is people don't exercise enough.
Jane	Quite.
Tom	I love football. I play every week and I always watch the matches on television. I think we need more football on TV!
Jane	Oh, I'm not so sure about that; there's usually one football match every week.
Tom	But there should be far more football, three or four matches at least!
Jane	I'm afraid I totally disagree with you. Maybe there should be more sports on TV but different things, too. Tennis is very exciting to watch.
Tom	But tennis is slow and boring on TV.
Jane	That's nonsense! Tennis matches are really good!
Tom	But football is the most popular sport in the world!
Jane	I'm afraid I can't quite agree with you about that.
Tom	But it is! If you think of the World Cup ...

b Now practise the dialogue in pairs. Take turns at being Tom and Jane.

2 Model Phrases

Follow the procedure outlined in the Introduction (page 5) about model phrases. Point out that there are two types of phrases for disagreement, those for disagreeing a little and those for disagreeing a lot. Remind students of the use of 'I'm afraid ...' to express 'I'm sorry'. Also, the words '... with you' are optional after the phrase 'I can't quite agree (with you)'.

3 Notes

a Tell the students to notice that the words 'Quite' or 'Right' are used not only to agree but also to show that the listener is willing for the speaker to continue speaking in the same way.

b Students staying in Britain might have already noticed that British people are often reluctant to disagree too strongly with another person's views and prefer to disagree in a milder fashion. Point out that it is easy to offend people by a disagreement which is too strong.

c These phrases for strong disagreement tend to be said mostly only in a heated argument or a debate and can often cause offence (see above) if used indiscriminately, in particular to people one does not know very well.

4 Pronunciation

Points to note:

a Slight stress on 'absolutely' and 'quite' with a falling intonation:

You're absolutely right.

I quite agree.

b Stress on 'think' with a rising intonation on 'so':

Oh, do you think so?

c The pronunciation of 'agree' [əgri] with a falling intonation:

I can't agree with you.

d The stress on 'totally' with a falling intonation:

I totally disagree.

e The pronunciation of 'nonsense' [nonsəns].

2 Model Phrases

a Agree

I quite agree.
Yes, of course.
Quite.
You're (quite) right.
You're absolutely right.

b Disagree a little

I'm not so sure about that. .
I'm afraid I can't quite agree (with you).
Oh, do you think so?

c Disagree a lot

I'm afraid I totally disagree.
I don't agree at all.
That's nonsense.
That's rubbish.

3 Notes

a These words are used to agree and also to encourage the speaker to continue speaking:

Quite/Right

b British people in general don't like to disagree too strongly so they use phrases such as:

I'm not quite so sure about that.
I'm afraid I don't quite agree (with you).
Oh, do you think so?

c These phrases are used only for expressing strong disagreement. You should be careful how you use them.

That's nonsense/rubbish.

4 Pronunciation

Now listen carefully and repeat.

5 Fluency Practice Exercises

a Divide the students into pairs and explain that one has to choose a
statement from the left-hand column and the other student has to
choose a suitable response from the right-hand column. There are
several possible responses to each item although it is only necessary
for the students to give one. The alternatives could be discussed after
they have completed the exercise.

5 Fluency Practice Exercises

a In pairs use the table to practise agreeing and disagreeing. One will make the statement and the other will reply. There are several possible answers.

I think computers are wonderful.	I quite agree.
Too many people smoke cigarettes.	That's nonsense!
Watching TV is fun.	You're absolutely right.
Everybody should learn English.	Yes, of course.
Pop music is terrible.	I'm not so sure about that.
People should stop working at 55.	I'm afraid I can't agree.
There's too much pollution.	Right.
Fruit is good for you.	That's rubbish!
Everyone should have six weeks' holiday a year.	Oh, do you think so?
Jogging is good for you.	I totally disagree.

b Divide the students into pairs and explain that one has to read the statement on the left and the other has to agree or disagree according to the instructions on the right. Tell them to take turns at this. Discuss the students' personal opinions after the exercise for further practice.

b Working in pairs one student will read the statements in the left column and the other will agree or disagree according to the instructions.

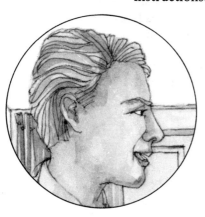

i	The theatre is more exciting than the cinema.	Agree
ii	It's stupid to wear a seatbelt in a car!	Disagree a little
iii	I think learning foreign languages is ridiculous!	Disagree a lot
iv	I think that sport is very good for you ...	Agree and show that you want him/her to continue
	... and it's also very interesting to watch.	
v	Sending rockets to the moon is a waste of money.	Disagree a little
vi	Young people need to learn more practical things at school.	Agree
vii	The most serious problem in the world today is crime.	Disagree a lot
viii	To be happy is more important than to have a lot of money.	Agree

6 Further Practice

Divide the class into small groups of three or four. Explain that the students have to note down four points under each heading (two examples are given in the Student's Book) and when they have done that discuss them with the other students in the group who must agree or disagree according to their opinions. Make sure they take turns at this and where time is limited give each student one topic only.

7 Situations

Please refer to the Introduction (page 7).

Suggested Answers

a I don't agree at all.
b You're absolutely right!
c I quite agree.
d I'm afraid I totally disagree.
e I'm not so sure about that.
f Yes, of course.
g I don't agree at all.

6 Further Practice

Write down four points about each topic below and then discuss them in turns in groups of three or four. The others will agree or disagree.
e.g. Flying is the safest way to travel.

   Here are two examples:
   i More accidents in a car.
   ii Better safety checks in planes.

Now you continue in the same way:

a Living in the city is better than living in the country.

b Television is better than the cinema.

c Everyone should stay at school until the age of 18.

7 Situations

a A friend tells you that all young people are lazy. Disagree.
b Someone you don't know very well says that pop music is terrible. Agree.
c A friend says that there is too much violent crime nowadays. Agree.
d A colleague says that the last department meeting was a waste of time. Disagree strongly.
e Computers will put everybody out of work in the end. Disagree slightly.
f Reading books and newspapers is better than watching TV. Agree.
g Men should not get married before they are 30. Disagree.

Unit 15   Problems and Sympathising

Everybody has problems from time to time – when a friend or acquaintance has a problem we need to express our sympathy or sorrow, and when we have one we need to know how to explain what's wrong. This unit aims to equip students of English with some basic phrases to perform this function in general conversation.

See Introduction for instructions on how to use each exercise.

Unit 15

Problems and Sympathising

1 Presentation

a Follow the procedure outlined in the Introduction (page 4) about relevant expressions. Before playing the cassette elicit from the class some simple problems which people might have in their everyday life, such as minor accidents, things lost, colds, etc. Explain that they will hear six short conversations in which a number of different people describe simple problems they have to friends who then sympathise with them. Pre-teach any unfamiliar vocabulary.

b Divide the students into pairs and tell them to practise reading the dialogues to each other, taking turns to be A and B.

2 Model Phrases

Follow the procedure outlined in the Introduction (page 5) about model phrases. Notice that the phrases are divided into asking about a problem and then sympathising.

1 Presentation

a Listen to the tape and fill in the spaces:

i   A: Hello, Roger, what's the matter? You don't look very well.

B: I don't feel well. I've got an awful cold.

A: I'm sorry to hear that.

ii   A: Did you know my wife is in hospital?

B: Oh dear, I am sorry. What's wrong?

A: She broke her leg skiing.

B: What a shame! I hope she'll be better soon.

iii   A: What's the trouble, Jane? You look very worried.

B: Yes, I've lost my passport.

A: Bad luck. Have you told the police?

iv   A: Is anything wrong? You look terrible.

B: I've got an awful headache.

A: Sorry about that. I hope you'll be better soon.

v   A: What's the trouble, Peter?

B: I failed my driving test this morning.

A: Oh, bad luck.

vi   A: My car's broken down.

B: Is there anything I can do?

A: Oh, yes. Could you give me a lift to the station?

b In pairs practise these dialogues. One will be A and the other B and take turns at this.

2 Model Phrases

a Asking

What's wrong?
What's the trouble?
What happened?
What's the matter? You look terrible.
Is anything wrong? / the matter? You don't look well.

b Sympathising

Oh dear, I am sorry.
I'm sorry to hear that.
Sorry about that.
What a shame!
Bad luck.
Is there anything I can do?
I hope you'll / he/she'll be/feel better soon.

3 Notes

Please refer to the Introduction (page 5).

4 Pronunciation

Points to notice:

a The rising tone of the questions in:

What's the matter?

What's wrong?

What's the trouble?

b The stress on 'sorry' and the falling tone in:

I'm sorry to hear that.

c The stress on 'I' and the pronunciation of 'can' [kən] in:

Can I help?

Is there anything I can do to help?

5 Fluency Practice Exercises

a Divide the students into pairs and tell them to make three-line dialogues using the phrases in the three boxes. The first student will choose a phrase from the first box, the second student will choose a problem from the second box, and then the first student will choose a suitable reply to sympathise from the third. Practise the example together first and do one or two others around the class to make sure the class understands the procedure. Note that although there is a wide variety of possibilities not all of the responses are suitable.

b In this exercise a number of problems are depicted in the illustrations and one student has to say what is wrong and the other has to sympathise accordingly. Notice that some words are given. Follow the procedure outlined in Unit 6, Part B, Exercise 5b (page 72).

3 Notes

When you ask 'What's the matter?' or 'What's wrong?' you often explain why, e.g.:
   What's the matter? You look tired.
   What's wrong? You don't look well.

4 Pronunciation

Now listen carefully and repeat.

5 Fluency Practice Exercises

a With a partner make short dialogues using this table for asking, giving the problem, and sympathising.

Here is an example:
   A: What's the matter?
   B: I've got a terrible headache.
   A: Oh, I'm sorry to hear that.

Asking	Problem	Sympathise
What's wrong? What happened? What's the matter? You don't look very happy. You look tired. What's the trouble? Is anything wrong? Is anything the matter?	I've lost my job. My car broke down. I've got a terrible headache. My mother/son is ill. I've got a bad cold. I'm worried about my job. I've just failed my driving test. I've had an argument with my boss/director.	Oh, I'm sorry to hear that. Is there anything I can do (to help)? What a shame! Bad luck. Oh dear, I am sorry. I hope you'll feel better soon.

b Work in pairs and look at the pictures. One student will say what the problem is and the other will sympathise. We have done the first one for you.

i A: I think I've got a temperature today.

   B: Oh, I'm sorry to hear that.

ii A: _____

   B: _____

iii A: _____

   B: _____

6 Further Practice

Divide the class into small groups and explain that they have to imagine they are patients waiting in a doctor's surgery. Discuss the kinds of problems people might have, examples of which are given in the book, to give the students some ideas and then tell them to think of their own problems. Tell each student to explain his/her problem to the others in the group who will sympathise. Students can also enquire about each other using the asking phrases, e.g. 'What's the matter ... you look terrible', etc.

7 Situations

Please refer to the Introduction (page 7).

Suggested Answers

a What's the matter ... you don't look very happy?
b What's the trouble?
c I'm sorry to hear that ... is there anything I can do?
d What happened?
e Oh, I am sorry ... can I help?
f Is there anything I can do?
g Can I help?
h I'm sorry to hear that.
i Bad luck.
j What happened?

iv A: _____

B: _____

v A: _____

B: _____

vi A: _____

B: _____

vii A: _____

B: _____

viii A: _____

B: _____

6 Further Practice

In small groups you are sitting in a doctor's waiting room and talking about your health problems. Each person has a particular problem or illness, e.g. you've got a bad cold; your baby has a fever, and the others must sympathise.

7 Situations

a You see a friend looking very unhappy. What do you say?
b You find a small child crying in the street? What do you say?
c Your friend tells you about his/her wife/husband in hospital. What do you say?
d You see a friend with a broken leg. What do you say?
e Your friend has a headache, sore throat, toothache and a bad cold. What can you say?
f You go to visit a friend who is in hospital after an accident. What do you say?
g You see someone looking on the floor for something. What do you say?
h A friend explains that they have moved to a new house but the neighbours are not very friendly. What do you say?
i Your brother/sister has just failed an examination at school. What can you say?
j You see a friend who has a black eye. What do you say?

Unit 16 Asking for and Giving Advice

From time to time everybody has a problem of one kind or another and we often ask advice from our friends and acquaintances, directly or indirectly, when we tell them our troubles. This unit aims to give students of English the necessary language not only to ask for advice but also how to give it to others.

See Introduction for instructions on how to use each exercise.

Unit 16

Asking for and Giving Advice

1 Presentation

a Follow the procedure outlined in the Introduction (page 4) about relevant expressions. Briefly discuss with the students the kind of everyday problems they might have both in their own country and when living abroad. Tell the students that they will hear eight short dialogues in which the first person mentions a problem or difficulty and the second person offers advice. Pre-teach any vocabulary which may be unfamiliar such as 'prescription', 'aspirin', 'urgently', 'purse' and so on. Point out that the table is in three columns – the first column is for the problem, the second column is for introducing the advice phrase, and the third column is the advice itself.

b Divide the class into pairs and tell them to practise the eight dialogues. One student will use the first column to explain the problem and the other will use the second and third columns to respond and give the advice. Make sure they take turns at this.

2 Model Phrases

Follow the procedure outlined in the Introduction (page 5) about model phrases.

a Asking for Advice

These phrases are used only to introduce a problem or actually ask for advice. Sometimes merely stating a fact such as 'I've got a cold' may produce a response with advice even though it was not directly asked for.

1 Presentation

a Listen to the tape and fill in the spaces:

	Problem	Advice phrase	Advice
i	ACHOO! I've got a terrible cold. ACHOO!	Why <u>don't you</u>	go to the <u>doctor's</u> and <u>get</u> a prescription?
ii	<u>I hate this</u> cold <u>weather</u>! What do you suggest?	<u>What</u> about	<u>going</u> to Greece? It's usually <u>warm</u> and <u>sunny</u> there.
iii	I've <u>got</u> an awful headache today.	If <u>I were you</u>	I'd <u>take</u> an aspirin. That might <u>help</u>.
iv	<u>My</u> car has <u>broken down</u> again so I had to <u>walk</u> to work.	<u>I think you should</u>	buy a new one.
v	<u>I need to</u> send this letter urgently. <u>What should I</u> do?	<u>You'd better</u>	send <u>it</u> by express delivery.
vi	<u>I've lost my purse</u> somewhere and I can't <u>find</u> it.	<u>I think you should</u>	<u>tell</u> the police. Someone may have found it.
vii	<u>I've run out of</u> milk and the shops are closed.	<u>What about</u>	<u>asking</u> your neighbour?
viii	I'm going <u>to a party</u> and I don't know what to take.	<u>Why don't you</u>	take some <u>flowers</u>? They're always suitable.

b Work in pairs and practise these dialogues. One will ask for advice and the other will give it. Take it in turns.

2 Model Phrases

a Asking for Advice

I've got this problem.
- What do you suggest?
- What (do you think) I should do?
- What can I do about it?

b Giving Advice

These phrases are virtually interchangeable.

3 Notes

Points to notice:

a The use of 'were' instead of 'was' in 'If I were you ...'
b The use of the infinitive without 'to' after 'You'd better ...'

You'd better see the doctor.
go to the hospital.

The use of the gerund after 'What about ...?' and 'How about ...?'

going to the cinema?
What/How about playing tennis?
having a holiday?

4 Pronunciation

Points to note:

a The pronunciation of 'can' [kən]:
What can I do about it?

b The contraction 'D'you' and the pronunciation of 'should' [ʃəd]:
What do you suggest?
What should I do?

The contraction of 'I would ...' and the pronunciation of 'were' [wə]:
If I were you I'd ...

c The rising intonation in:

What about talking to the manager?

How about going to the dentist?

5 Fluency Practice Exercises

a Divide the class into pairs and explain that they have to ask for and give advice alternately. Tell them to look at the tables before beginning the exercise so that they are familiar with the problems and responses. Explain any unfamiliar vocabulary such as 'cough', 'optician', etc. and tell the students that there is generally only one suitable answer. Practise one or two examples all together before doing the exercise in pairs. Make sure they take turns at this.

b Giving Advice

Why don't you I think you should You'd better If I were you I'd	talk to the boss? see the doctor? go to the chemist's?
What/How about	going to the doctor's? changing it? talking to the manager?

3 Notes

a If I were you I'd ... (*Not* If I was you I'd ...)

b Notice the structure in these phrases. We use the infinitive verb without 'to':

If I were you I'd Why don't you I think you should Perhaps you'd better	go to the doctor's.

But after these phrases we use the '-ing' form of the verb:

What about How about	going to the doctor's?

4 Pronunciation

Now listen carefully and repeat.

5 Fluency Practice Exercises

a With a partner use the tables to ask for and give advice and take turns at this.

Asking

> I've got a headache. What can I do about it?
> I've broken my glasses.
> I lost my cheque book yesterday. What should I do?
> What should I do about my cough?
> My neighbours are so noisy!
> What should I do about my holidays?
> What should I do about these new shoes? They don't fit.
> I've missed the last train!
> I don't know what to do about my car. It won't start.
> I've got a bad back.
> I need a birthday present for my grandmother. What do you suggest?
> My telephone's not working. What should I do about it?

b Divide the class into pairs and explain that the pictures show different problems. One student has to say what is wrong and the other has to advise accordingly.

Advising

If I were you I'd You'd better Why don't you I think you should How about What about	take some cough medicine. go to the travel agency. contact the bank. see the doctor. take it to the garage. go to the optician in the High Street. asking the police about it. go back to the shop and change them. get a taxi. use mine. book a room in a hotel. buying some flowers. write a letter to complain. have an aspirin.

b Working in pairs look at the pictures which show different problems. One student will explain what the problem is and the other will give advice. We have done the first one for you.

i A: I've got terrible backache.

B: Why don't you go to the doctor's?

ii A: _____

B: _____

iii A: _____

B: _____

iv A: _____

B: _____

6 Further Practice

a Before they begin discuss things that the students may want to know when planning a visit to another country. Some ideas are given in the Student's Book to establish the pattern. Divide the class into pairs of different nationalities if possible and tell them to ask for advice and give advice in turns about a projected visit to each other's country. Where students are all of the same nationality tell them to imagine they are foreigners visiting their own country for the first time.

b This is an extension of Part 6a and pairs should be arranged as above. In this situation, however, the students have to imagine they are in their partner's country for the first time and are discussing problems they might have. Talk about the kinds of difficulties they might encounter before they start and again use the examples in the book to establish the pattern.

7 Situations

Please refer to the Introduction (page 7).

Suggested Answers

a If I were you I'd go to the Indian restaurant/La Tavernetta/etc.
b Why don't you go to Harrods/Brown's Boutique?
c How about going to Italy/Peru?
d You should go to Debenham's department store ... and the Odeon cinema has good films ... and you can join the sports centre ... and the buses are very good during the week ...
e You'd better go to the Lost Property Office.
f If I were you I'd get some cough mixture.
g Why don't you go to Edinburgh/Canterbury ...?
h I think you should write a strong letter of complaint.
i You'd better go to the police station and report it.

6 Further Practice

a Somebody is planning a trip to your country and asks about the best methods of travel, time of year, places to go, what to bring, souvenirs, etc. Work in pairs and one student will ask for advice and the other will give it. Take turns at this, e.g.:

> A: When is the best time to come?
> B: I think you should come in the spring.
> A: What type of clothes will I need?
> B: If I were you I'd bring a raincoat and some sweaters.

b One person has come to your country for the first time and is discussing problems he/she has. Give advice about the problems and take turns at this, e.g.:

> A: I don't understand what people say in the shops.
> B: Why don't you ask them to speak more slowly.
> A: I don't know the best places to visit at the weekend.
> B: How about going to the Tourist Information Office?

7 Situations

a A friend wants to go to a good restaurant in your town. Advise him/her where to go.

b Somebody asks you for advice about somewhere to go in your town to buy fashionable clothes. What do you advise?

c You are planning to go on a holiday abroad. Ask a friend for advice.

d A new family has just moved into the apartment next door. Advise them about shops, cinemas, sports facilities and local transport.

e A friend has left her shopping on a train. Advise her what to do.

f Someone with a bad cough asks you for advice. What do you say?

g A friend asks you about interesting places to visit at the weekend. What do you advise?

h A friend asks for advice about a problem with neighbours playing loud music late at night. What do you say?

i A friend's bicycle was stolen at the Sports Centre. Advise him/her what to do.

Unit 17   Apologising and Complaining

It is often necessary to apologise for something one has done by accident and this unit aims to teach students to be able to say they are sorry and also how to respond when apologised to. It is also important to be able to complain about poor service and conditions, and the language to perform this function is also incorporated into the unit.

See Introduction for instructions on how to use each exercise.

1 Presentation

a Follow the procedure outlined in the Introduction (page 4) about relevant expressions. Discuss with the students the kinds of everyday situations where they would have to apologise, such as stepping on someone's foot or spilling something, and the kinds of situations where they would need to complain about something, such as poor service in a restaurant or an incorrect bill in a shop. Explain that they will hear eight short dialogues – in the first four (i–iv) people are apologising for things that have happened and suitable replies are given; in the next four (v–viii) people are making complaints about things and replies are also given. Many of these may have occurred in the earlier discussion. Pre-teach any unfamiliar vocabulary such as 'bill', 'spill', 'charged', etc.

b Divide the class into pairs and tell them to practise the dialogues, taking it in turns to apologise/complain and respond.

Unit 17

Apologising and Complaining

1 Presentation

a Listen to the tape and fill in the spaces:

Apologise	Response
i Oh, I'm awfully sorry. I've broken a glass.	Oh, well, . . . never mind.
ii Oh, I'm terribly sorry. I've spilt my coffee on the carpet.	Oh, don't worry. We can clean it up
iii Sorry I'm late but I missed the bus.	Well, how on earth did that happen?
iv I'm awfully sorry but I'm afraid I had an accident with your car.	What! You should be more careful.

Complain	Response
v Waiter, I'm afraid this food is cold.	I'm terribly sorry. I'll change it immediately
vi I bought a new TV last week and it doesn't work. There's no picture at all.	I'm very sorry to hear that.
vii I'm afraid there's a mistake in the bill. You've charged me for three bottles, not two.	I'm extremely sorry about that.
viii I'm afraid I have a complaint to make. This cassette doesn't work properly.	Oh, I'm very sorry. Let me change it.

b Work in pairs and practise these dialogues. One will apologise or complain and the other will reply. Take it in turns.

2 Model Phrases

Follow the procedure outlined in the Introduction (page 5) about model phrases.

a Apologising

It is possible to say only 'I'm sorry' but the adverbs are often used to emphasise the apology.

b Complaining

'I'm afraid' can be used to mean 'I'm sorry' as mentioned in previous units but only to introduce something unpleasant one is about to say. It is not an apology.

3 Notes

a Point out the difference between phrases used when you are not angry and when you are and note that although in general British people are fairly slow to lose their tempers and the anger is being conveyed by the intonation in what is said (see 4 Pronunciation) it is not always the case.

b These responses are for when someone apologises to you for something minor they have done.

4 Pronunciation

Points to note:

a The stress on 'very', 'terribly' and 'awfully' with a falling tone in:

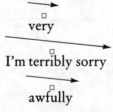

very

I'm terribly sorry

awfully

b The rising intonation for the question and the stress on 'that' in:

Oh, how did that happen?

Oh, how did you do that?

2 Model Phrases

a Apologise

			Response
	extremely		It's O.K.
	very		That's all right.
I'm	terribly	sorry.	It doesn't matter.
	awfully		Don't worry.
			Oh well, never mind.

Sorry.

How on earth did that happen?
How did you do that?
What! You should be more careful!

b Complaining

I'm afraid ...
I'm sorry but ...
I'm afraid I have a complaint to make ...

3 Notes

a After an apology:

  i If you are not angry you can say:

    That's all right.
    Never mind.
    It's O.K.

  It is very common to say 'Oh well ...' at the beginning of this type of sentence to show we are not angry, e.g.:

    Oh well, never mind.

  ii If you are angry or not pleased you can say:

    (Oh!) How on earth did that happen?
    (Oh!) How did you do that?
    What! You should be more careful!

b If you step on someone's foot or bump into someone you say:

	Response
Sorry	That's all right.
I'm sorry	O.K., don't worry.

4 Pronunciation

Now listen carefully and repeat.

5 Fluency Practice Exercises

a Divide the students into pairs and tell them they have to use the table to apologise and complain from the left-hand column and respond from the right-hand column. Allow time for them to study the table and explain that all the responses are not possible although there may be more than one alternative for each statement or question. Make sure that the students take turns at using each side of the table. When they have finished discuss which responses are suitable for each item from the left-hand side.

b Divide the class into pairs and explain that the pictures show what one student has just done. (A brief revision of the Present Perfect with 'just' would be useful before beginning this exercise.) One student has to say what has happened and then apologise and the other has to respond accordingly.

5 Fluency Practice Exercises

a With a partner use the tables for apologising and complaining and choose suitable responses. Take turns at this.

I'm afraid I've broken a glass.	Oh well, don't worry.
Could you give me back the book I lent you last week.	I'm very sorry, sir/madam.
I'm afraid I've had an accident with your stereo.	I'm afraid I missed the bus.
I'm sorry but I forgot to post that letter for you.	I'm extremely sorry about that – I'll change it.
I'm afraid this watch I bought here doesn't work.	How on earth did that happen?
Where were you last night? I waited outside for an hour.	I'm awfully sorry. I've lost it.
I'm sorry I'm late.	How did you do that?
Sorry.	I'm terribly sorry about that.
I'm afraid there's a mistake on the bill.	It doesn't matter.
I'm afraid I have a complaint to make.	What! You should be more careful!

b Working in pairs look at the pictures. One student must explain what he/she has done and then apologise and the other must respond. We have done the first one for you.

i A: Oh, I've spilt coffee on your carpet.

B: Oh, how did that happen?

ii A: _____

B: _____

iii A: _____

B: _____

iv A: _____

B: _____

v A: _____

B: _____

vi A: _____

B: _____

6 Further Practice

The situation in the illustrations generates various opportunities to complain and apologise. Divide the students into pairs or small groups and explain that they have to take the part of the manager or the guest(s) in a hotel. The two rooms in the hotel have several faults which the guests complain about. Before looking at the picture discuss briefly some of the problems that there might be in a hotel room and use this discussion to pre-teach as much vocabulary as is necessary for the exercise, such as 'dripping tap', 'unmade bed', etc. Tell each pair/group to study the pictures and work out what to say. This could be exploited in a number of ways:

i as a straightforward oral practice exercise

ii as a written exercise with the students writing out the dialogue between the manager and guest(s) and then 'acting' it out for the rest of the class

iii as a recorded exercise on cassette or video camera (where possible) which could be played back to the rest of the class for critical appraisal afterwards

6 Further Practice

Look at these two pictures of a hotel room. In pairs or small groups one
will be the manager and the other the guest(s). The guest(s) must
complain about the problems in the rooms and the manager must
apologise.

7 Situations

Please refer to the Introduction (page 7).

Suggested Answers

a I'm awfully sorry.
b I'm terribly sorry I'm late – I got held up in the traffic.
c I'm afraid I have a complaint to make. This cassette recorder that I bought this morning doesn't work properly.
d I'm extremely sorry but I scratched the record you lent me.
e I'm afraid I have a complaint to make . . . this food doesn't taste good.
f I'm sorry but I can't sleep with all this noise you're making!
g I'm very sorry . . . let me clean it up.
h Sorry.
i I'm very sorry I'm late but my car broke down.
j I'm afraid there's a mistake in the bill.
k I'm terribly sorry.
l Sorry.

7 Situations

a You've just upset a cup of coffee on the carpet. What do you say?

b You arrive half an hour late for a business appointment. Apologise and explain.

c You bought a cassette recorder in a shop and when you got it home it didn't work properly. Complain to the shop assistant.

d You borrowed a record from a friend and accidentally scratched it. What do you say?

e You are having lunch in a restaurant and the soup tastes horrible. Complain to the waiter.

f The people in the flat next to you are playing loud music. It's three o'clock in the morning and you can't sleep. Complain to them.

g You knock over a vase of flowers at a friend's house. What do you say?

h You're walking along a crowded street and you bump into someone. Apologise.

i You arrive at the dentist's forty-five minutes late. What do you say?

j You're shopping in a supermarket and when you check the bill you find a mistake. Complain to the manager.

k You're sitting on a train and your shopping bag falls onto the person sitting beside you. What do you say?

l You accidentally stand on someone's foot in the bus queue. What do you say?

Unit 18   Congratulations and Compliments

We all need to congratulate our friends and acquaintances from time to time or compliment them on something they have done, the way they look or something new they have bought and this unit aims to provide students with the necessary language to do this.

See Introduction for instructions on how to use each exercise.

Unit 18

Congratulations and Compliments

1 Presentation

a Follow the procedure outlined in the Introduction (page 4) about relevant expressions. Discuss with the students when they would congratulate or compliment somebody. Explain that they will hear nine short dialogues in which the speakers congratulate or compliment people on a variety of things and pre-teach any vocabulary which may be unfamiliar.

b Divide the students into pairs and tell them to practise the nine dialogues and take turns with the different parts.

1 Presentation

a Listen to the tape and fill in the spaces:

i	A: Have you heard? Margaret and I are going to get married. B: That's great! Congratulations!
ii	A: What a beautiful dress. You look very smart. B: Oh, thank you very much.
iii	A: What do you think of my new car? B: I think it's marvellous.
iv	A: I've just won a holiday to New York! B: Congratulations! I'm so pleased.
v	A: Hello, Mike. B: Hello, Brian. By the way, congratulations on your new job in London. A: Thanks very much. I'm looking forward to it.
vi	A: Mmmm ... that was delicious. You're a very good cook. B: Oh, thank you. I'm glad you enjoyed it.
vii	A: I really like your new flat. It's very comfortable. B: Thanks very much. I'm pleased you like it.
viii	A: I've just passed my driving test. B: Well done! Congratulations!
ix	A: Janet and I are getting engaged. B: Congratulations! I'm delighted to hear about that. A: Thank you very much.

b Work in pairs and practise these dialogues. One will be A and the other B and take turns at this.

2 Model Phrases

Follow the procedure outlined in the Introduction (page 5) about model phrases.

a This list is for congratulations which are generally offered when one has been told by another person about something they have done or achieved.

b These phrases are for compliments which can be asked for, e.g. 'What do you think of my new car?' or for spontaneous compliments when one is particularly impressed by somebody's appearance, ability, etc.

3 Notes

The preposition 'on' is used when 'Congratulations' is followed by a noun or noun phrase.

'Well done' is used only for an achievement, not an emotional or family event.

2 Model Phrases

a Congratulations

Congratulations on your   engagement.
new job.
exam results.

Congratulations!

I'm (so)   happy
pleased   (to hear) about that.
delighted

That's   great.
fantastic.
marvellous.

Well done!

b Compliments

What a   wonderful
lovely   car/dress/book/baby/picture.
beautiful

I think it's   marvellous.
super.
great.

I (really) like your (new)   car.
apartment.
suit.

That was   delicious.
excellent.
wonderful.

c Response

Thank you.
Thank you very much.

3 Notes

a If somebody asks 'What do you think of … ?' or 'Do you like my … ?' you can answer:

I think it's lovely/wonderful/great.

b If somebody has done something good, e.g. got a new job, passed an exam or won a prize, you can say:

Congratulations!

4 Pronunciation

Points to note:

a The stress on 'lovely' in:
  What a lovely new dress.

b The stress on 'really' in:
  That's really great.

c The pronunciation of the first syllable of 'congratulations' [kən].

d The stress in:
  You look very smart.
  That was wonderful.

5 Fluency Practice Exercises

a Divide the students into pairs and explain that they have to make statements or ask questions from the left-hand column and respond from the right-hand column in turns. Tell them that there may be several possibilities although not all the responses are suitable. Discuss the alternatives when the students have finished.

You don't need to repeat the activity in your response but if you introduce the subject, e.g. a wedding, you can say:

Congratulations on your wedding.

c If you want to compliment somebody without being asked you can say:

You look very nice/smart/elegant.
I like your new shirt/shoes/trousers.
What a nice hat/watch/car.

d After you have eaten a meal that was very good you can say:

That was delicious.

e When people get engaged or married or have a baby you can say:

Congratulations on your   engagement.
                                        marriage.
                                        new baby.

You do not say 'Well done' in these cases.

4 Pronunciation

Now listen carefully and repeat.

5 Fluency Practice Exercises

a Work in pairs. One will give the phrases on the left and the other will reply from the column on the right. Take turns at this. There may be several suitable replies.

I've just got engaged.	Well done.
I passed my driving test!	Congratulations. I'm so pleased.
Do you like my new jacket?	I'm delighted to hear that.
What do you think of my new motorbike?	Congratulations! I hope you'll be very happy.
I've won a trip to Mexico.	It looks very smart.
What an elegant pair of shoes.	That's great.
I've just got a new job.	I think it's fantastic.
Have you heard about my new baby daughter?	That's absolutely marvellous.
I've just passed my final exams.	Thanks very much.

b Divide the students into pairs and explain that the pictures illustrate various achievements/exciting events, etc. One student has to explain what has just happened and the other has to congratulate him/her.

b Working in pairs look at the pictures. Take it in turns to congratulate or compliment each other according to the picture. We have done the first one for you.

i A: I've just passed my driving test!

B: Well done! Congratulations!

ii A: _____

B: _____

iii A: _____

B: _____

iv A: _____

B: _____

v A: _____

B: _____

vi A: _____

B: _____

6 Further Practice

a Divide the class into groups of five or six students and explain the situation in which a VIP is giving prizes to people who have done amazing things and then congratulating them. Discuss some possible achievements, which can be as unusual as the students like, and then tell them to take turns at being the announcer (A), the Important Person (B), and the person with the prize (C), according to the example. Groups could perform their prize-giving ceremonies for the rest of the class for general appraisal.

b Divide the class into pairs and explain that one of them has to be the boss and the other the employee. Before they begin discuss compliments an employee might pay his/her boss, which can be as amusing as the students like, in order to obtain a pay rise. Tell them to think of five compliments and to take turns at being the boss and the employee.

7 Situations

Please refer to the Introduction (page 7).

Suggested Answers

a Well done! That's wonderful!
b Congratulations! I'm so pleased about it.
c I think it's very fashionable.
d That was really delicious.
e What a terrific motorbike.
f That's marvellous ... well done.
g I think he's/she's beautiful.
h Congratulations on your new job!
i I really like your shirt – is it new?

6 Further Practice

a Work in groups. One student will be an important guest who is giving prizes to people who have done amazing things and congratulating them. Another will be the announcer and the rest of the group must think of things they could have done, e.g.:

A = Announcer   B = Important guest   C = Guest

A: This is Mr Jones who has just swum across the Mediterranean!
B: That's fantastic! Congratulations!
C: Thanks very much.

b Work in pairs with one student as the boss and the other as an employee. The employee wants a pay rise from the boss and must think of five compliments for the boss in order to persuade him/her to give them the rise, e.g.:

A: Oh, Mr Miller, what a smart tie you're wearing.
B: Thanks very much.

7 Situations

a A friend tells you he/she has just won first prize in a competition. What do you say?
b A colleague has recently got married. What do you say when you meet him/her?
c A friend asks what you think of her new dress. What do you say?
d You have just had an excellent dinner at a friend's house. What do you say?
e A friend shows you a new motorbike he has recently bought. What do you say?
f A friend has just won a tennis match at the local Sports Centre. What do you say?
g A colleague shows you a picture of his/her new baby? What do you say?
h A relative has just been promoted to the New York Sales Office. What do you say?
i You see a friend wearing a beautiful new shirt. What do you say?

Revision Units 13 – 18

This revision unit has recall exercises for the last six units although the other earlier twelve units may also be needed for some of the situations. If necessary go over the language taught in the relevant units in question to refresh the students' memories before doing the six activities.

1 Music Questionnaire

The language of asking for and giving opinions (Unit 13) is featured in this activity. Divide the class into small groups and explain that each student has to make up a questionnaire along the lines of the cutaway questionnaire given in the Student's Book. The names of the other students in the group should be put at the top of the questionnaire and three more sections should be added to the questions column. Discuss with the class the kinds of things they might ask about pop music – which could include the names of singers, about music in public places – which could include supermarkets, stations and so on. Check the questionnaires when the students have drawn them up and tell them to interview the others in their group and write down the answers. When they have finished tell the students to explain the results to the rest of the class following the examples given in the Student's Book.

Revision Units 13 – 18

Unit 13   Asking for and Giving Opinions
Unit 14   Agreeing and Disagreeing
Unit 15   Problems and Sympathising
Unit 16   Asking for and Giving Advice
Unit 17   Apologising and Complaining
Unit 18   Compliments and Congratulations

1 Music Questionnaire

In small groups find out the opinions of the other students about music. On a piece of paper prepare a questionnaire like the example below and make three more sections about pop music, musical instruments and music in public places. Use the phrases from Unit 13 for asking for and giving opinions to help you, e.g.:

What's your opinion of . . .?
Do you like . . .?
What do you think of . . .?

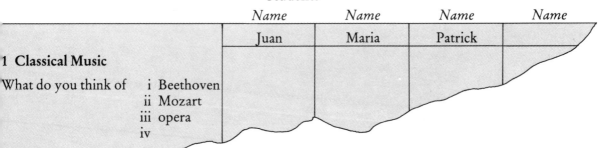

	Students			
	Name	*Name*	*Name*	*Name*
	Juan	Maria	Patrick	
1 Classical Music				
What do you think of i Beethoven				
ii Mozart				
iii opera				
iv				

Explain the results to the rest of the class, e.g.:

Juan thinks Beethoven is marvellous.
Maria doesn't like pop music at all.
Patrick likes the guitar.

2 Personal opinions

Divide the students into pairs. Tell the students to choose one of the four topics, and ensure that each student in a pair chooses a different topic. Explain that they have to think of five reasons in favour of the subject chosen and write them down in note form. When they have finished tell the students to discuss their topics together using the phrases from Unit 13 to express their opinions and to ask for the opinions of their partner, and to agree and disagree (Unit 14) accordingly.

3 Giving Advice

This activity uses the language of problems and sympathising (Unit 15) and asking for and giving advice (Unit 16). The situation is that of a Council Advice Office which gives advice on problems people have. Elicit from the class the sort of problems and worries people might discuss in such an office, e.g. money, neighbours, local authorities, house repairs, etc. Divide the students into pairs and tell them to think up problems they might have at home. When they are ready divide them into 'clients' and 'advisers' and tell them to act out these roles with one student talking about his/her problems while the other responds sympathetically and gives suitable advice. The teacher could arrange the room appropriately and give the students special names to make the role play more realistic. Where possible this exercise could be recorded on video camera while they are acting out the scenario. Each pair should reverse roles to give them both practice in the relevant language.

2 Personal Opinions

Working in pairs choose one of the four topics below. One student must think of five reasons against and the other must think of five reasons for the topic, and then discuss it together. Use the phrases in Unit 13 for Giving Opinions and Unit 14 for Agreeing and Disagreeing.

Smoking should be forbidden in public places.
People should retire at 55.
Everybody must stay at school until they are 18.
Everybody should do military service.

3 Giving Advice

Council Advice Office

Problems?

Worries?

Troubles?

Questions?

Office Hours: 1000 – 1600, Monday – Friday
26 Grimley Gardens   phone 56491

Come in – no appointment necessary

In pairs prepare a short list of problems you might have at home, at work, with the local council, with money, etc. Then take your problems to the Council Advice Office. One student will be the client with the problems and the other will be the adviser. Take turns at this.

Clients – tell the office about your problems and ask for advice and suggestions.
Advisers – sympathise with your clients and give them suitable advice.

Use the phrases from Unit 15 for Problems and Sympathising and 16 for Asking for and Giving Advice to help you.

4 Problems with the Neighbours

This exercise provides practice in the language for problems and sympathising (Unit 15) and apologising and complaining (Unit 17). First tell the students to imagine they live in the block of flats depicted in the Student's Book and ask them to imagine the problems generated in such a situation. Discuss the difficulties which might be encountered with neighbours who live in such a block of flats, drawing if possible on their personal experiences. When they have studied the pictures divide them into pairs or small groups of 'angry tenant' and 'neighbour(s)' and tell the tenant to go to the neighbour(s) and complain about the problems and give a reason why it disturbs him/her. The others have to respond by apologising for the nuisance that caused the problem and sympathise with the difficulty. The students could also supplement this exercise by drawing another block of flats with problems of their own invention to give further practice.

4 Problems with the Neighbours

Look at this picture of the block of flats:

Imagine you live in this block of flats. Go to the neighbours and
complain about the problems they are causing and they will apologise.
Work in pairs and one will complain and the other will be the neighbour
and apologise. Take turns at this. Use the phrases in Unit 15 and Unit 17
for Apologising and Complaining to help you.

5 Compliments

This activity practises the phrases for compliments in Unit 18. Divide the students into pairs and explain that one of them is a salesperson and the other is a prospective customer. Discuss various possible products as well as the examples in the book and ways of selling them through different compliments, e.g.:

a Attractive hair would need a good shampoo, so the salesperson could say:

   What a pretty hairdo! You need our shampoo.

b A smart dresser would need a good iron, so the salesperson could say:

   What a lovely dress/shirt! Why don't you buy this wonderful iron!

Tell them to compliment each other and try to sell the product. Discuss the various ideas at the end and choose the most imaginative ones.

6 Congratulations

This activity revises the phrases used for congratulations in Unit 18. Give each student a card and tell him/her to write on it two things as shown in the Student's Book.

a Point out that this should be about another student in the room which can be real or imaginary.

b This is about an event, real or imaginary, in his/her own life.

Remind them to put their own names on the card. Collect the cards when they have finished and put them in a hat or box for the students to choose from, or distribute them in a similar way. Tell each student to read out the card to the class and then congratulate the people concerned who should respond accordingly.

5 Compliments

Work in pairs with one student as a salesperson trying to sell something to the other student. Think of a product, e.g. new washing powder, video, etc., and try to sell it to your customer by complimenting him/her on appearance, clothes, hairstyle, etc., e.g.:

> What a beautiful dress . . . you look very smart. You need a good washing powder to keep it really clean!

Use the phrases in Unit 18 for Compliments and Congratulations to help you.

6 Congratulations

Each student must write the following things on a card:

a A reason, real or imaginary, to congratulate another student in the room.

b An exciting event or happening of his/her own, e.g.:

> **a** Maria has just got engaged.
> **b** I (name) have just passed my driving test.

The teacher will collect the cards and then give them out to other students who will read them and congratulate the people on them.

Use the phrases from Unit 18 for Compliments and Congratulations to help you.

Tapescripts

Unit 1   Meetings and Introductions

1   i   **Tom**   Hello, my name's Thomas.
      Barbara   Hello, I'm Barbara.
      Tom   Where are you from?
      Barbara   I'm from Bristol. What about you? Where do you come from?
      Tom   I'm from Edinburgh.

  ii   **Jane**   This is Maria. She's from Spain. Maria, this is John.
      John   Hello, Maria, nice to meet you.
      Maria   Hello, John.

  iii   **Mary**   John, I'd like you to meet Mr Walker. Mr Walker, this is John Fraser, the office manager.
      Mr Walker   How do you do.
      John   How do you do.

  iv   **Joan**   Mr Snell, I'd like to introduce you to the president, Mr Rogers. Mr Rogers, this is Mr Snell.
      Rogers   How do you do, Mr Snell, nice to meet you. Please call me Roy.
      Snell   How do you do, Mr Rogers, nice to meet you too. And please call me Rob.

4   Hello ... my name's ... my name's Bob ...
Hello, my name's Bob ... my name's Mary ... Hello, my name's Mary.
Hello ... I'm Fred ... Hello, I'm Fred ... Hello, I'm Jane ...
Where ... are you from? ... Where are you from ... ?
Where ... do you come ... do you come from? ... Where do you come from?
This is John ... This is Jenny ... This is Mark ... This is Sue.
Nice to meet ... Nice to meet you ...
I'd like ... I'd like you to meet ... I'd like you to meet Mr Brown ... I'd like you to meet Mrs Peterson ...
I'd like ... to introduce you ... I'd like to introduce you ... I'd like to introduce you to Mr Milne ... I'd like to introduce you to Miss Harris ...
How ... do you do ... How do you do ...

Unit 2   Talking about Yourself

1   **Selina:**   Hello, my name's Selina.
      Richard: Hello, I'm Richard. Where are you from?
      Selina: From Canada. What about you?
      Richard: I'm from England.
      Selina: Are you here on holiday?
      Richard: No, on business.
      Selina: What do you do?
      Richard: I'm an engineer. What about you?
      Selina: I'm an accountant. Where do you live in England?
      Richard: In Oxford. Do you know it?
      Selina: No, I don't.
      Richard: It's a lovely town. I live there with my wife and family.
      Selina: How many children have you got?
      Richard: Three girls. What about you. Are you married?
      Selina: No, I'm single.
      Richard: Oh, I see. Are you here on holiday?
      Selina: Yes, I am. I'm interested in Italian art.
      Richard: What about your other hobbies?
      Selina: Well, I'm very interested in cooking and playing chess.
      Richard: I see. I like chess, too. Well, excuse me but I must go. I'm going to a tennis match now.
      Selina: Oh, I'm interested in tennis, too.

4   I'm ... I'm from Spain ... I'm from Italy ... I'm from Saudi Arabia ... I'm from Turkey.
I come from ... I come from Paris ... I come from Tokyo ... I come from Stockholm ... I come from Geneva.
I'm interested ... I'm interested in music ... I'm interested in football ... I'm interested in collecting stamps.
I've got ... I've got two children ... I've got a baby and two dogs.
Where ... are you from? ... Where are you from?

What ... do you do? ... What do you do?
What about ... What about you?

Unit 3   Giving Yourself Time to Think

1   i A: What's the date today?
       B: Er ... it's the twenty-seventh.

   ii A: When are you going to Paris?
       B: Just a moment while I check in my
          diary ... it's next Friday.

  iii A: How many people are coming to the
          party?
       B: Now ... let me see ... it'll be twenty-
          four altogether.

   iv A: How much is a return ticket to
          London?
       B: Well, I'm not quite sure ... ten
          pounds I think.

    v A: What's the name of the shop where
          you bought that book?
       B: Um ... let me think ... Smith's ...
          yes, that's it ... Smith's.

   vi A: What time is the football match on
          TV?
       B: Just a minute ... it's at three forty-
          five

  vii A: Where is the Chinese restaurant?
       B: Er ... I'm not quite certain ... I think
          it's on the third corner.

 viii A: When is the company party?
       B: Just a moment ... it's on July the
          twenty-first.

4 Just a ... Just a moment ... Just a moment
   while I ... Just a moment while I look ... look
   in my diary ... while I look in my diary ...
   Just a moment while I look in my diary.
   Now ... let me ... let me see ... Now, let me
   see ... Now, let me think ...
   I'm not ... quite sure ... I'm not quite sure ...

Unit 4   Not Understanding

1   i A: Could you tell me the time, please?
       B: It's achoo ... achoo ... three.

      A: Pardon ... I didn't quite catch that.
      B: I said it's half past three.

   ii A: (very fast) There's a good film on TV
         tonight.
      B: I'm sorry, I can't understand what
         you're saying.
      A: There's a good film on TV tonight.

  iii A: How much does it cost to send a letter
         to Spain?
      B: It's ... cough ... cough ... pence.
      A: Sorry?
      B: It's twenty-four pence.

   iv A: What's your phone number?
      B: (very quietly) It's double six-five-
         seven-nine.
      A: Could you repeat that, please?
      B: It's double six-five-seven-nine.

    v A: (Background noise) Could I have
         your address, please?
      B: (More noise) Yes, it's 146 Rook
         Road.
      A: Sorry, I didn't catch that.
      B: It's 146 Rook Road.

   vi A: (On the telephone ... interference)
         Could I speak to Ms Harris, please?
      B: (Crackle ... crackle ...) Could you
         speak up, please?
      A: Could I speak to Ms Harris, please?

  vii A: (Dog barking) Where are you going
         for your holidays?
      B: I'm going to (bark ... bark) ...
      A: Sorry, I didn't quite catch that.
      B: I'm going to Austria.

 viii A: (Pop music on juke box) What would
         you like to drink?
      B: I'd like (loud music ...).
      A: Pardon ... could you speak up,
         please?
      B: (Shouting above music) I'll have a
         lager, please.

4 Pardon ... your pardon ... I beg your
   pardon.
   Could you ... Could you speak up ... Could
   you speak up, please ... more slowly ...
   Could you speak more slowly, please?

I didn't ... I didn't quite ... I didn't quite catch that.
I'm sorry ... I can't understand ... I'm sorry, I can't understand ... what you're saying ... I can't understand what you're saying ... I'm sorry, I can't understand what you're saying.

Do you know ... where the cinema is? ... Do you know where the cinema is?
Yes ... go straight on ... Yes, go straight on ... it's on the left ... Yes, go straight on and it's on the left.
No ... I'm sorry ... No, I'm sorry ... No, I'm sorry I don't.
No ... I'm afraid ... No, I'm afraid ... No, I'm afraid I can't.

Unit 5 Asking for and Giving Information

1 i A: Excuse me, could you tell me the time, please?
      B: Yes, of course. It's ten fifteen.

   ii A: Excuse me, do you know when the bank opens?
      B: Yes, it opens at nine thirty.

   iii A: Excuse me, can you tell me where the cinema is?
      B: Yes, go straight on ... it's on your right.

   iv A: Hello, can you tell me the dialling code for Brighton, please?
      B: Yes, it's oh-two-seven-three.

   v A: Do you know where the British Airways check-in desk is, please?
      B: No, I'm afraid I don't.

   vi A: Excuse me, could you tell me where I could buy a postcard near here, please?
      B: Yes ... in the little shop there on the corner.

   vii A: Excuse me, do you know where the bank is?
      B: Sorry, no. I'm a stranger here myself.

   viii A: Excuse me, can you tell me when the supermarket opens?
      B: Yes, of course. It opens at eight thirty every morning.

4 Excuse me ... could you ... Excuse me, could you ... could you tell me ... Excuse me, could you tell me ... could you tell me the time, please ... Excuse me, could you tell me the time, please.
Yes ... Yes, of course ... it's three o'clock ... Yes, of course, it's three o'clock.

Unit 6 Asking for Things
Part A Food and Drink

1 i A: Good afternoon, sir. What can I get you?
      B: I'd like a cup of coffee, please.
      A: Yes, certainly, sir.

   ii A: Would you like to order?
      B: I'll have chicken and chips, please.
      A: Certainly.

   iii A: Can I have two Cokes, please?
      B: Yes, of course. Here you are.
      A: Thank you very much.

   iv A: Could I have a hamburger, please?
      B: Yes, certainly. Anything else?
      A: No, that's all, thanks.

   v A: Could you pass me the butter, please?
      B: Yes, of course. Here you are.
      A: Thanks.

   vi A: I'd like a packet of peanuts, please.
      B: Here you are. Anything else?
      A: Umm ... A packet of crisps, too, please.
      B: Certainly.

   vii A: What would you like for dessert?
      B: Could I have chocolate ice cream, please?
      A: Yes, of course.

   viii A: Could you pass the salad dressing, please?
      B: Certainly. Here it is.
      A: Thank you.

4 I'd like ... I'd like a Coke, please ... I'd like a hamburger, please.

I'll have ... I'll have a salad, please ... I'll have coffee please.
Can I have ... Can I have a cup of tea, please? ... Can I have chicken, please?
Could I have ... Could I have a glass of orange juice, please? ...
Could I have a rare steak, please?
Could you pass ... Could you pass me ... Could you pass me the salt, please? Could you pass me the bread, please?

Part B Shops and Services

1   i   A: May I have a dozen eggs, please.
        B: Of course. Here you are.
        A: And could I have some cheese, please?
        B: I'm sorry but we've run out of cheese.

   ii   A: Have you got an English dictionary?
        B: Yes, what sort would you like?

  iii   A: I'd like some grey shoes, please.
        B: Yes, what size do you want?

   iv   A: Could I have five stamps for letters to Saudi Arabia, please?
        B: Mmmm ... anything else?
        A: And I want to send two postcards to France.
        B: Certainly, here you are.

   v   A: Hello, I'd like to change these travellers' cheques, please.
        B: Certainly.

   vi   A: Have you got a local newspaper, please?
        B: No, I'm afraid I haven't.

  vii   A: Have you got any batteries for clocks, please?
        B: I'm sorry but we haven't.

  viii   A: I'd like a long woollen scarf, please.
        B: Certainly. What colour?

4 Have you ... Have you got ... Have you got any ... Have you got any blue shirts? ... Have you got any red shoes?
May I ... May I have ... May I have some ... May I have some eggs, please? ... May I have some air mail paper, please?

I'd like ... I'd like a film for my camera, please ... I'd like a packet of biscuits, please.
Could I ... Could I have ... Could I have a tube of toothpaste ... Could I have some shampoo, please?

Unit 7   Making Offers, Accepting and Refusing

1   i   A: Would you like a Coke?
        B: Yes, please, I'd love one.

   ii   A: Would you like a cup of coffee?
        B: No, thanks, not just at the moment.

  iii   A: How about some pudding?
        B: Yes, please, I'd love some.

   iv   A: Can I get you a sandwich?
        B: That's very kind of you, thanks.

   v   A: Let me help you with that heavy suitcase.
        B: Thanks, but it's all right.

   vi   A: How about a piece of chocolate cake?
        B: Yes, please, I'd love one.

  vii   A: Can I help with the dishes?
        B: No, thank you, I can manage.

  viii   A: Would you like some biscuits?
        B: No, thanks, not right now.

4 Would you ... Would you like ... a cup of tea ... Would you like a cup of tea?
How about ... How about some cake? ... How about a Coke?
Yes, please ... I'd love one ... Yes, please, I'd love one.
very kind ... That's very kind ... That's very kind of you.
No, thanks ... not at the moment ... No, thanks, not at the moment.
not right now ... No, thanks, not right now.
Not for me ... Not for me, thanks.

Unit 8   Invitations

1   i   A: Would you like to go out for dinner on Friday, Anne?
        B: That's very kind of you, Tom. I'd love to.

ii A: Are you free to come to the disco with me tonight, Jane?
   B: Yes, please. I'd love to.

iii A: Would you like to come to my party on Saturday evening?
   B: That's very kind of you but I'm afraid I can't.

iv A: Do you want to come to London with us at the weekend?
   B: Thanks for asking me but I'm afraid I can't.

v A: Would you like to play tennis this afternoon?
   B: That would be very nice, I'd love to.

vi A: Are you free to come for a picnic on Saturday afternoon?
   B: Thanks for the invitation but I'm afraid I can't.

vii A: Would you like to see the new art exhibition after work tomorrow?
   B: Yes, I'd love to.

4 Would you ... Would you like ... Would you like to come ... Would you like to come to dinner? ... Would you like to go to the cinema? ... Would you like to play tennis?
That's ... That's very kind ... That's very kind of you ... I'd love to ... That's very kind of you, I'd love to.
I'm sorry ... but I can't ... I'm sorry but I can't.
I'm afraid ... I'm busy ... I'm afraid I'm busy then.
Thanks for asking me ... but I can't ...
Thanks for asking me but I can't.

Unit 9   Asking for Permission

1   i A: Is it all right if I close the window?
     B: Yes, of course.

   ii A: Is it possible for me to use your telephone?
     B: No, I'm afraid you can't ... it's out of order.

  iii A: Could I borrow your pen?
     B: By all means.

iv A: Would it be possible for me to arrive late for work tomorrow, Mr Parker?
   B: I'm sorry but you can't. That would be the second time this week.

v A: Do you think I could turn off the radio?
   B: Certainly, please do.

vi A: Is it all right if I smoke?
   B: I'd rather you didn't.

vii A: Could I sit here?
   B: I'm sorry but this seat is taken.

viii A: May I leave early this afternoon?
    B: Yes, that's all right.

ix A: Can I switch on the light? It's a bit dark.
   B: Yes, of course. Go ahead.

4 Can I ... Can I open ... Can I open the window?
Is it ... Is it all right ... Is it all right if I use ... Is it all right if I use your phone?
May I ... May I use ... May I use your pen?
Yes ... Yes, of course.
That's ... That's all ... That's all right.
Certainly ... Certainly, please do.
I'd ... I'd rather ... I'd rather you didn't.
No ... No, I'm afraid ... No, I'm afraid you can't.
I'm sorry ... I'm sorry but ... I'm sorry but I need it.

Unit 10   Likes and Dislikes

1 **Jane:** Would you like to listen to some Beethoven?
Tom: Yes, please. I love classical music.
Jane: So do I. I like Beethoven very much. I'm fond of pop music, too.
Tom: Are you? I'm not.
Jane: Aren't you? Oh, I love it. I'm very keen on musical films, too.
Tom: So am I. I enjoy a good Western as well.
Jane: Oh, do you? I don't. I can't stand them because of the violence. I like romantic films.

Tom: So do I, especially the good old-fashioned ones.

4 A: I like ... I like playing ... I like playing tennis.
B: So do I.
A: I enjoy ... I enjoy cycling.
B: Do you? ... I don't ... Do you? I don't.
A: I'm fond of ... I'm fond of walking.
B: So am I.
A: I'm keen on ... I'm keen on football.
B: Are you? ... I'm not ... Are you? I'm not.
A: I hate ... I hate shopping ... I hate shopping for food.
B: Do you? ... So does John ... Do you? So does John.
A: I can't ... I can't stand ... I can't stand writing ... I can't stand writing letters.
B: Nor can I ... Neither can I.

Unit 11 Telephoning

1 i A: Bournemouth five-one-seven-five-six.
B: Could I speak to Frances, please?

ii A: Hello.
B: Hello, could I speak to Mr Black, please?
A: This is Mr Black speaking.
B: This is Mrs Walker.

iii A: Hello.
B: Hello, can I speak to Liz, please?
A: I'm sorry, she's out now. Is there any message?
B: Could you tell her John rang?
A: All right.

iv A: Good morning, Royal Park Hotel. Can I help you?
B: Good morning. Could I speak to Mr Charles King, please? He's in Room five-two-six.
A: Who's calling please?
B: This is Mrs King.
A: Hold on, please.

v A: Hello, Pascoe's Office Supplies.
B: Hello, could I speak to Mrs Grant, please?
A: I'm afraid she's not available at the moment. Who's calling?

B: This is Mr Freeman of Newton and Company. Could you ask her to call me back?
A: Yes, certainly, Mr Freeman. Goodbye.

4 Could I ... Could I speak to ... Could I speak to Mr Smith ... Could I speak to Mr Smith, please?
This is ... This is Mr Smith ... This is Mr Smith speaking.
I'll call ... I'll call back later.
Who's calling ... Who's calling please?
Hold on ... Hold on a minute ... I'll get her ... Hold on a minute, I'll get her ... Hold on a minute, I'll get her.
Can you give ... Can you give him a message ... Can you give him a message, please?
I'm sorry ... Mrs Turner isn't available ... I'm sorry, Mrs Turner isn't available.

5 b
i (*Ring ... ring ... ring*)
A: Hello, five-eight-oh-nine-six.
B: Could I speak to Janet, please?
A: I'm sorry but she's out. Would you like to leave a message?
B: Could you ask her to phone Mrs Brandon this evening, please?
A: Yes, of course. Goodbye.

ii (*Ring ... ring ... ring*)
B: Parker and Company. Can I help you?
A: Could I speak to Mr Mansfield, please?
B: Who's calling, please?
A: This is Les Winter speaking.
B: Hang on. I'm sorry, Mr Mansfield isn't in his office at the moment. Is there any message?
A: Could you ask him to call me as soon as possible? My number is eight-double-three-two-six-three.
B: Yes, of course. Goodbye.
A: Goodbye.

iii (*Ring ... ring ... ring*)
B: Good morning. Regal Cinema.
A: (Pause for Student)
B: This week it's *Rocky Three*.
A: (Pause for student)
B: At two fifteen/four twenty-five/six forty-five and nine o'clock.
A: (Pause for student)

B: At about eleven fifteen.
A: (Pause for student)

iv (*Ring . . . ring . . . ring*)
B: Good evening. Tavernetta restaurant.
A: (Pause for student)
B: Certainly, what time?
A: (Pause for student)
B: I'm sorry but we're completely booked then. But I can give you a table at six forty-five or at eight fifteen.
A: (Pause for student)
B: Certainly, and how many people?
A: (Pause for student)
B: Mmm . . . and the name, please?
A: (Pause for student)
B: Thank you. We look forward to seeing you on Saturday.

Unit 12   Instructions

1 **Tom:** I'd like to know how to make a good pot of tea. What do you do first?
Jane: Well, first of all you have to fill the kettle with fresh water and boil it, of course.
Tom: Oh, yes (laugh) . . . and then?
Jane: Then you put a little hot water in the teapot to warm it.
Tom: And next?
Jane: Next you put in the tea.
Tom: Mmmmmm . . . how much?
Jane: A teaspoonful for each person and one for the pot.
Tom: What's next?
Jane: When the water is boiling you pour it into the teapot.
Tom: Right. And then?
Jane: Then you let the tea stand for a couple of minutes.
Tom: What do you do next?
Jane: Last of all you drink it . . . with sugar and milk or lemon.

4 First . . . First of all . . . First of all you add the tea. Last . . . Last of all . . . Last of all you put in the milk.
The first . . . The first thing . . . The first thing you add . . . is the tea . . . The first thing you add is the tea.

You make . . . You make it . . . You make it like this.
Next . . . Next you leave it.
And then . . . And then you add . . . And then you add the sugar.

Unit 13   Asking for and Giving Opinions

1   i A: What do you think of people smoking in restaurants?
B: I think it's terrible.

ii A: What's your opinion of children wearing school uniforms?
B: Well, I don't think they should really.

iii A: Do you think children should get pocket money?
B: Well, I'm afraid I don't, really.

iv A: What do you think of national military service?
B: I think it's a very good idea.

v A: Do you think watching TV is bad for children?
B: Well, it's not too bad.

vi A: What's your opinion of driving at age sixteen?
B: I really don't think they should.

vii A: Do you like the idea of voting at age eighteen?
B: Yes, I do. I think it's a good idea.

viii A: What do you think about the drug problem nowadays?
B: In my opinion it's terrible.

4 D'you . . . D'you think . . . D'you think people should smoke . . . in public places . . . Do you think people should smoke in public places?
D'you . . D'you like . . . Do you like my new car?
I think . . it's fantastic . . . I think it's fantastic.
What . . . What d'you think . . . What d'you think of the film . . . What d'you think of smoking?
What's your opinion . . . What's your opinion of children . . . What's your opinion of children watching TV?

Unit 14 Agreement and Disagreement

1 Tom: Well, Jane, I think sport is good for you and everybody should take exercise.

Jane: I quite agree, Tom.

Tom: Too many people sit in their offices all day. They don't get out and do anything to keep fit!

Jane: You're absolutely right.

Tom: The main reason for heart attacks is people don't exercise enough.

Jane: Quite.

Tom: I love football. I play every week and I always watch the matches on television. I think we need more football on TV!

Jane: Oh, I'm not so sure about that; there's usually one football match every week.

Tom: But there should be far more football, three or four matches at least!

Jane: I'm afraid I totally disagree with you! Maybe there should be more sports on TV but different things, too. Tennis is very exciting to watch.

Tom: But tennis is slow and boring on TV.

Jane: That's nonsense! Tennis matches are really good.

Tom: But football is the most popular sport in the world!

Jane: I'm afraid I can't quite agree with you about that.

Tom: But it is! If you think of the World Cup . . . (fade out)

4 You're . . . You're absolutely . . . You're absolutely right.
I quite . . . I quite agree.
Oh . . . d'you think . . . d'you think so? . . . Oh, d'you think so?
I'm afraid . . . I'm afraid I can't . . . I'm afraid I can't agree . . .
I'm afraid I can't agree with you.
I totally disagree . . . I totally disagree with you.
Nonsense . . . That's nonsense.
Rubbish . . . That's rubbish.

Unit 15 Problems and Sympathising

1 i **A:** Hello, Roger, what's the matter? You don't look very well.
 B: I don't feel well. I've got an awful cold.
 A: I'm sorry to hear that.

 ii **A:** Did you know my wife is in hospital?
 B: Oh dear, I am sorry. What's wrong?
 A: She broke her leg skiing.
 B: What a shame! I hope she'll be better soon.

 iii **A:** What's the trouble, Jane? You look very worried.
 B: Yes, I've lost my passport.
 A: Bad luck. Have you told the police?

 iv **A:** Is anything wrong? You look terrible.
 B: I've got an awful headache.
 A: Sorry about that. I hope you'll be better soon.

 v **A:** What's the trouble, Peter?
 B: I failed my driving test this morning.
 A: Oh, bad luck.

 vi **A:** My car's broken down.
 B: Is there anything I can do?
 A: Oh, yes. Could you give me a lift to the station?

4 What's . . . What's the matter?
What's . . . What's wrong?
What's . . . What's the trouble?
Is . . . Is anything . . . Is anything wrong?
I'm sorry . . . to hear that . . . I'm sorry to hear that.
Is there . . . Is there anything . . . I can do . . . Is there anything I can do to help?

Unit 16 Asking for and Giving Advice

1 i **A:** ACHOO! I've got a terrible cold. ACHOO!
 B: Why don't you go to the doctor's and get a prescription?

 ii **A:** I hate this cold weather! What do you suggest?

B: What about going to Greece? It's usually warm and sunny there.

iii A: I've got an awful headache today.
B: If I were you I'd take an aspirin. That might help.

iv A: My car has broken down again so I had to walk to work.
B: I think you should buy a new one.

v A: I need to send this letter urgently. What should I do?
B: You'd better send it by express delivery.

vi A: I've lost my purse somewhere and I can't find it.
B: I think you should tell the police. Someone may have found it.

vii A: I've run out of milk and the shops are closed.
B: What about asking your neighbour?

viii A: I'm going to a party and don't know what to take.
B: Why don't you take some flowers? They're always suitable.

4 Do you think ... What do you think ... What do you think I should do?
Do you suggest ... What do you suggest?
Don't you ... Why don't you ... go to the doctor ... Why don't you go to the doctor?
If I were you ... I'd go ... If I were you I'd go ... I'd go by train ... If I were you I'd go by train.
I think ... I think you should ... buy another one ... I think you should buy another one.
What about talking ... to the manager ... What about talking to the manager?
How about going ... to the dentist ... How about going to the dentist?

ii A: Oh, I'm terribly sorry. I've spilt my coffee on the carpet.
B: Oh, don't worry. We can clean it up.

iii A: Sorry I'm late but I missed the bus.
B: Well, how on earth did that happen?

iv A: I'm awfully sorry but I'm afraid I had an accident with your car.
B: What! You should be more careful!

v A: Waiter, I'm afraid this food is cold.
B: I'm terribly sorry. I'll change it immediately.

vi A: I bought a new TV last week and it doesn't work. There's no picture at all.
B: I'm very sorry to hear that.

vii A: I'm afraid there's a mistake in the bill. You've charged me for three bottles, not two.
B: I'm extremely sorry about that.

viii A: I'm afraid I have a complaint to make. This cassette doesn't work properly.
B: Oh, I'm very sorry. Let me change it.

4 I'm ... I'm very ... I'm very sorry ... I'm terribly ... I'm terribly sorry ... I'm awfully ... I'm awfully sorry.
That's ... That's all right.
It doesn't ... It doesn't matter.
Oh ... how ... Oh, how on earth ... did that happen ... Oh, how on earth did that happen?
How did you do ... How did you do that?
more careful ... You should be ... You should be more careful ...
What! ... What! You should be more careful!
I'm afraid ... I'm afraid I have ... I'm afraid I have a complaint.
I'm sorry ... I'm sorry but ... it doesn't work ... I'm sorry but it doesn't work.

Unit 17 Apologising and Complaining

1 i A: Oh, I'm awfully sorry. I've broken a glass.
B: Oh, well, never mind.

Unit 18   Congratulations and Compliments

1   i A: Have you heard? Margaret and I are going to get married.
       B: That's great! Congratulations.

   ii A: What a beautiful dress. You look very smart.
       B: Oh, thank you very much.

  iii A: What do you think of my new car?
       B: I think it's marvellous.

   iv A: I've just won a holiday to New York!
       B: Congratulations! I'm so pleased.

    v A: Hello, Mike.
       B: Hello, Brian. By the way, congratulations on your new job in London.
       A: Thanks very much. I'm looking forward to it.

   vi A: Mmmm ... that was delicious. You're a very good cook.
       B: Oh, thank you. I'm glad you enjoyed it.

  vii A: I really like your new flat. It's very comfortable.
       B: Thanks very much. I'm pleased you like it.

 viii A: I've just passed my driving test.
       B: Well done! Congratulations.

   ix A: Janet and I are getting engaged.
       B: Congratulations! I'm delighted to hear about that.
       A: Thank you very much.

4 That's ... That's fantastic.
  Congratulations ... on your engagement ...
  Congratulations on your engagement.
  I think ... I think it's ... I think it's great.
  I'm delighted ... I'm delighted about that.
  You look ... You look very smart.
  What a ... What a lovely ... What a lovely dress.
  Wonderful ... That was wonderful.
  Delicious ... That was delicious.